AMERICAN PLACES

A Profile of Local Economies Across the U.S.

JAY SHABAT

American Places
A Profile of Local Economies Across the U.S.

ISBN 979-8-9882128-0-5

Published by: Railroad Weekly

Contents

About the Author

Jay Shabat studied economic policy at Columbia University's School of International and Public Affairs (SIPA), and international business at The George Washington University before that. After several years as a pricing and revenue management analyst for US Airways and Air France, he launched and later sold a newsletter about the global airline industry. He continues to write about airlines today, and about the railroad industry and the U.S. economy as well. He is also the co-author of "Glory Lost and Found: How Delta Climbed from Despair to Dominance in the Post-9/11 Era." You can follow him on LinkedIn at https://www.linkedin.com/in/jay-shabat-6477b31/.

Foreword

My interest in economics goes all the way back to middle school and high school. I was lucky to have had talented teachers who sparked my appetite to learn more and more about the subject. Even today, when I contemplate why a city is wealthy, or why a company is failing, or why inflation is too high, the words of my seventh-grade history teacher Mr. Koskuba still ring in my head: "Always establish cause and effect."

What causes the economies of some places in America to thrive but others to struggle? That's a focus of this book, which is a collection of economic profiles I wrote between January 2021 and June 2022. I originally published them for a newsletter I wrote called Econ Weekly (which you can still read at https://www.econweekly.biz/). Every Monday, it featured a summary of the latest developments in the U.S. economy, ranging from corporate earnings to policy decisions in Washington to the latest data on unemployment and inflation. One section looked deeper at individual companies and another that did the same for specific sectors. Still another covered financial markets. One section described economic trends outside the U.S. One covered government policy. And so on. Each week, I also looked at development of economic importance from America's past (i.e., the evolution of its monetary system, or how the country financed conflicts like the Civil War). I also wrote about developments potentially important for the future (like artificial intelligence or autonomous vehicles). But most enjoyable for me? Selecting a place—a city, a state, a county, even a neighborhood—and trying to dissect and explain its economy.

Later, I returned to writing exclusively about transportation, but not before publishing 71 U.S. place profiles. During 2021 and 2022, of course, all of America was managing the impact of a deadly pandemic. The crisis impacted the economy in dramatic ways, from the extraordinary stimulus measures taken by Congress and the Federal Reserve to the crushing blow it had on industries like aerospace, tourism and downtown office real estate. On the other hand, the crisis was not a crisis at all for most industries. In fact, the U.S. economy, after adjusting for inflation, grew almost 6% in 2021, propelled by thriving industries like housing, energy, retail, finance, manufacturing, agriculture, logistics and information technology. Stock markets soared. So did bond markets. So did the value of pretty much all financial assets—don't forget about SPACs, meme stocks, and crypto-coins. The unemployment rate, which reached nearly 15% in April 2020, dropped below 4% by the end of 2021.

The job market would stay strong throughout 2022. But problems arose. Inflation was the biggest one, driving the Federal Reserve to repeatedly raise borrowing costs. This immediately halted the housing boom, as well as the stock and bond boom. Speculative asset markets crashed. Supply chain bottlenecks and high energy costs would remain a headache through much of 2022. Still, GDP grew a more or less healthy 2% for the year. For that credit ongoing strength in consumer spending, in turn supported by the strong job market and elevated savings (some still left over from Washington's stimulus measures). In addition, in-person service industries hammered by the pandemic, led by leisure, hospitality, travel, medical care, and education, reversed course and returned to health. As I write this forward in March of 2023, the U.S. economy continues to defy recession fears, though fears persist. The housing and IT sectors appear to be shrinking. Inflation is off its 2022 highs but still uncomfortably rising. The consumer goods economy has softened. Out of the blue, a bank in Silicon Valley collapsed. The Fed is warning of more interest rate hikes to come.

You'll encounter many of the leading pandemic-era economic trends as you read about the places featured in this book. You'll see, for example, how different areas across the country grappled with a surge in housing prices during 2021—it was great for homeowners but a major problem for home *buyers*. Affordable housing scarcity was a major problem too for economic development officials seeking to recruit companies and workers. Other trends prevalent throughout this book include the importance of health care, education, and government to local employment, the burdensome legacy cities still face from post-war deindustrialization and suburbanization, the effects of more people working from home rather than in downtown offices, the important role that logistics companies like Amazon have played in creating new jobs, the challenges of America's aging demographics… And so on.

You'll also see how economies across America are shaped by a vast constellation of forces, among them history, geography, technology, government policies, corporate strategies, entrepreneurship, and even geopolitics. Why is Silicon Valley so rich but the Mississippi Delta so poor? How did some cities like New York recover from de-industrialization but others like Baltimore did not? How does a remote place in coastal Alaska maintain a healthy economy? How about a Native American reservation, or other places still scarred by a legacy of unjust treatment. How about a place economically dependent on prisons or coal mines or steel mills? What about those dependent on federal transfers, be it military spending or social security checks? Many American places, you'll quickly see, are greatly dependent on what some call "eds and meds," meaning education and health care institutions.

How did I choose these 71 places? Rather randomly, to be frank. Some are places I've lived in or visited. Some are places that I simply wanted to know more about. Occasionally I'd ask friends for recommendations on what they'd like to read about. My friend and former colleague Madhu Unnikrishnan, for example, told me about Susanville, California. Seth Kaplan and Brian Streeval gave me lots of good ideas. So did Andrew Young, with whom I recorded an Econ Weekly podcast each week. There are really too many people to acknowledge, so I'll stop there. In any case, I tried to pick places from different parts of the country, some thriving economically, some struggling, and others in between. I also tried to pick places with varying demographic profiles.

Wherever the focus, it quickly becomes clear that the American economy is really a collection of many economies: vibrant economies, dying economies, emerging economies, economies heavily and lightly regulated, economies with large and limited government influence… This mix is on display throughout the country, from the fisheries of Alaska to the skyscrapers of New York City.

Naturally, some of the profiles—especially those early in the book—don't include important events that occurred more recently. An example is the brutal hurricane that ravaged much of Lee County, Florida, in September 2022. Tech giants aren't hiring like they were when portions of this book were written. The housing market has cooled. Ditto for freight transportation. As of this writing in March 2023, however, there's nothing in this book that makes any of the profiles obsolete. Or at least I hope not, though that's for you to judge. I hesitate to make any promises, but my hope is that you'll read this book and come away thinking: I now have a better understanding of how the American economy functions, as it's experienced by different people in different places. Even better if you also come away thinking: I found this book interesting and enjoyable.

I dedicate "American Places" to the economic leaders across the country, whose efforts are helping to achieve what Jefferson wanted for Americans: that they be free to pursue happiness. Is there any higher calling?

-Jay Shabat, March 2023

About the sources used for this book:
Most of the data, quotes, and other information used to write this book are cited as I go along. For many of the profiles, local economic development officials were instrumental in helping me understand the area's job market, housing market, fiscal situation, and so on. You'll see frequent citations of information from the U.S. Census and the U.S. Department of Housing and Urban Development. The latter's Comprehensive Market Analysis reports were super helpful. Think tanks and policy centers provided lots of useful information. Same with industry associations. For airline, rail transport, and general travel—my own areas of expertise—I often used data from Cirium, Airlines for America, the Association of American Railroads, and my own employer Skift. More generally, this book is the product of ideas, learnings and conclusions I've drawn from the many articles, books, podcasts and speeches I've consumed about the U.S. economy, especially during my time writing Econ Weekly.

(1)

LEE COUNTY, FLORIDA

January 2021

Lee County, Florida, is in many ways perfectly representative of an American sunbelt boom city. Located on Florida's Gulf Coast, covering the Fort Myers/Cape Coral metro area, the county's population grew by roughly 20% from 2010 to 2020. And that's despite getting hammered by the housing crisis of 2008. Not long after, however, the influx of people resumed. America's swelling mass of retiring baby boomers, many from midwestern states like Minnesota and Ohio, came for the sun. Some came for the affordable housing and other aspects of low-cost living, including the absence of personal income taxes for Florida residents. Jobs became plentiful, notably in tourism, health care, retail, and anything to do with housing—selling them, building them, fixing them, furnishing them, financing them, insuring them... Like most medium-sized population clusters across America, Lee County depends heavily on "eds and meds" for employment (education and health care, in other words). The county's non-profit hospital network and school system, indeed, are its two largest employers, accounting for about 25k jobs between them. Two competing supermarkets—Publix and Wal-Mart—are Lee County's next largest employers. Local government functions including law enforcement employ large numbers as well. The biggest private sector employer with its headquarters in Lee County? That would be Chicos, a clothing retailer. Also large is the IT research firm Gartner. Another big resident is Hertz, the recently-bankrupt but now-revived rental car company that moved from New Jersey a few years ago. How did Lee County perform during the Covid shock? Unsurprisingly, the area's large tourist sector was hit hard. But not as hard as some other leisure-oriented places. In October, 2020, for example, the Fort Myers airport saw just a 35% y/y drop in passenger volumes, compared to a 64% decline nationwide. In 2021, the housing market caught fire again, boosting the construction sector along with it. Tourism revived sharply as well. Throughout the pandemic, the region's many retirees (almost 30% of residents are over 65) continued to receive their social security checks, providing an important anchor of stability for the local economy.

ST. LOUIS, MISOURI

January 2021

I f southwest Florida exemplifies a booming American sunbelt mecca, St. Louis represents something less flattering. In fact, it's sometimes used as a case study in how *not* to govern a metro area. The city was a rock star of the 1800s, rising from a humble French trading outpost to America's fourth largest city by 1900. It saw large waves of German and Irish immigrants. It was an important Union base during the Civil War. It's the symbolic gateway to the west, hence the iconic Gateway Arch monument towering along the Mississippi River. The Mississippi of course, made St. Louis an important river port when river ports greatly mattered. It became a vibrant railway hub as well. By 1880, it had the country's third largest cotton market. Meatpacking and shoemaking were important. The city even played a key role in financing and developing Mexico's late 19th century industrialization, according to Henry W. Berger's book "St. Louis and Empire." Even in the first half of the 20th century, the two World Wars—notwithstanding the Depression in between—created lots of new demand for St. Louis manufacturers. But the city's population would drop from 900k people in 1950 to a mere 300k today. What happened? For one, Chicago became a far more important railway hub, and later one of the country's busiest airline hubs. Well into the 20th century, St. Louis remained uncomfortably dependent on river commerce, which lost much of its relevance as railways and later highways expanded. Buffalo and Cincinnati, incidentally, were two other U.S. boom towns sent into decline as river commerce gave way to rail commerce, according to Colin Gordon, author of the 2008 book "Mapping Decline: St. Louis and the Fate of the American City." Gordon, though, highlights another key reason for the city's decline: Bad public policies. The U.S. Constitution, he notes, doesn't mention anything about municipal forms of government, just state government. But Missouri's state government is in Jefferson City. St. Louis wanted to make its own decisions about matters close to home. So in 1875, the state granted it "home rule." Well, St. Louis is still regretting the move today. The problem is that suburban areas around the city also won home rule, boxing St. Louis into its relatively small geographic footprint. St. Louis can't just annex territory to expand like many other U.S. cities can. In those budding suburbs, meanwhile, federal mortgage loan guarantees that began in the 1930s encouraged real estate developers to create incorporated self-governing towns beyond city limits. The new towns would adopt "deed covenants" that typically barred dirty industries and non-White residents. Both, alas, remained left behind in St. Louis proper while middle class White residents and more modern businesses—with their tax dollars—flocked to the suburbs in droves. The city of St. Louis itself became older, poorer, and Blacker. Compounding the problem were counterproductive attempts later to lure back residents; building expressways through the city certainly didn't help. So why not create a single entity to govern the entire St. Louis metro area, optimizing what's best for city and suburbs alike? Does it really make sense for a single region—with a shared economy—to have 12 counties, more than 100 municipalities, and over 200 other government entities (school districts, sewer districts, museum authorities, etc.)? As it happens, there *was* a major effort in 2019 to merge St. Louis County with St. Louis the city. It ultimately fizzled. What's the St. Louis metro area economy like today? Its population currently ranks 20th in the country with about 2.8m people, surpassed a few years ago by much faster-growing Denver. Of the nation's 50 largest metro areas, St. Louis ranks 45th measured by population *growth* during the 2010s—it grew less than 1% last decade. To this day, few major metros have a larger share of residents living outside city limits. It's still home to some big multinational firms like Emerson Electric, the health insurer Centene, and the agribusiness firms Bunge and Monsanto. Washington University is a leading employer. But many of the area's top corporate names were swallowed by companies from elsewhere: Boeing bought McDonnell Douglas. Nestle bought Ralston Purina. American Airlines bought TWA. InBev bought Anheuser Busch. Cigna bought Express Scripts. Mallinckrodt Pharmaceuticals, meanwhile, filed for bankruptcy this fall, swamped by litigation tied to its role in distributing opioids. Peabody Coal filed in 2016. Most of these companies, however, continue to operate and employ many area residents. Others like Dallas-based Southwest Airlines have expanded their St. Louis footprint. The area remains a major center of aerospace and auto manufacturing, along with pharmaceuticals and agribusiness. It's been less successful attracting information technology jobs (notwithstanding native son Jack Dorsey of Twitter fame). It's also not a terribly large tourist destination (notwithstanding the famous Arch).

(3)

BOSTON, MASSACHUSETTS

February 2021

Yale historian Mark Peterson, in his 2020 book "The City-State of Boston," chronicles the origins of one of America's oldest cities, from its founding in 1630 to the end of the Civil War in 1865. A central theme is that the city early on—an independent-minded trading hub not unlike Singapore today—actually scarified its independence and economic interests by supporting the U.S. Federal Constitution. That's because the new central government amplified the power of southern interests, often at Boston's expense. Virginia, in particular, dominated federal politics in the early years of the Republic, notwithstanding the presidency of Massachusetts native John Adams. In the earliest days, Boston hardly seemed destined for fortune. It lacked good farmland. Natural resources were few. Activities like fur trading and fishing were insufficient to support the population. The real action among Europe's 17th century colonies was in the Caribbean islands growing sugar, or in areas of Latin American with gold or silver. Eventually, Boston took advantage by developing trade with the islands, while defying its British overlords and developing a local currency based on silver coins from Potosi in Peru (then the largest city in the Americas). Boston traded with Europe too, and shipping became a staple of its economy. It was very much active in the slave trade. Boston, of course, would revolt against Britain, epitomized by the 1773 Tea Party. Shortly after the Revolutionary War, though, Peterson's point about losing influence to Virginia became evident. In 1807, the city's shipping sector was hit hard by President Jefferson's trade embargo, a precursor to the War of 1812 with Britain. New England even discussed secession. But after the war, textile manufacturing (producing clothes) would supersede shipping in importance, facilitated by the advent of railroads as a means of distribution. Textiles were the dominant product of the industrial revolution, much like automobiles would assume a similar role in the post-WWII era. But just as autos required oil, the dominant commodity of the 20th century, textiles required cotton, the commodity at the center of America's pre-Civil War economy (and the global economy more broadly). Where did the Boston area's textile mills get their cotton? From the southern slaveocracy, of course. Historians call it the alliance between the "lords of the loom" and the "lords of the lash." The relationship was an uneasy one, complicated by New England's support for high tariffs (to dampen competition from British clothing imports) and the South's support for low tariffs (because it feared retaliation from Britain and other countries that bought its cotton). Tariffs, then the chief revenue source for Washington, would be a source of great tensions between the north and south in the decades preceding the Civil War. Boston, meanwhile, in the two decades prior to the war, experienced great demographic change with a mass influx of Irish immigrants. The city was home to a sizeable African American population too, and a strong abolitionist movement. Yet Peterson writes that it was America's most racially segregated city by 1860. After the war, Boston lost much of its manufacturing edge as emerging industries like railroads and steel developed elsewhere. Textile production would move to places with cheaper labor. Its political relevance reawakened with the Kennedy family in 20th century. In the 21st, it's attained a highly favorable position in the global economy, with world-class universities, hospitals, tech companies and wealth management firms. Moderna, now famous for producing a Covid vaccine, is based in the Boston metro. So are Fidelity (investment), Raytheon (defense) and the conglomerate General Electric (aviation, health care, etc.).

(4)

SILICON VALLEY, CALIFORNIA

February 2021

In northern California, on a peninsula abutting the Pacific Ocean, you'll find towns like Palo Alto, Menlo Park, Mountainview, Santa Clara and Cupertino. Together, sandwiched between San Francisco to the north and San Jose to the south, they form what's come to be called Silicon Valley, one of the richest places on earth. It's also of course, synonymous with the tech economy, and home to giants like Google, Apple, Facebook, Netflix, Intel and Tesla (before it moved its headquarters to Austin, anyway). How did this area of northern California become the epicenter of so many world-changing companies? Margaret O'Mara offers some answers in her 2019 book "The Code: Silicon Valley and the Remaking of America." Prior to World War II, Palo Alto was a sleepy railway village perhaps best known for the surrounding valley's prune farming. There was Stanford University, named after railroad magnate Leland Stanford. There was also Hewlett-Packard, an electronics company founded in 1939. The world war, and the cold war that followed, saw a massive jump in government spending on technologies relevant to national defense and space exploration. That meant lots of money for universities like Stanford and companies like Lockheed, an aerospace giant in southern

California, which moved parts of its operation to the Valley. The real break-through, however, came in the 1960s with the advent of silicon transistors from AT&T's Bell Labs in New Jersey. As O'Mara writes, these would become for electronics what oil had become for automobiles. All sorts of new applications emerged, including, eventually, personal computers. Boston's "Route 128" was an early leader in developing applications for these silicon chips. But Silicon Valley had cheap hydro-energy from government-built damns, lots of real estate to develop industrial parks and visionary leadership at Stanford. In 1965, President Johnson signed the Hart-Celler immigration act, which O'Mara calls "one of the most consequential economic policies of the latter half of the 20th century." By the 1980s, a third of the Valley's new companies had founders from either India or China. The fall of the Soviet Union would usher in another wave of talent in the 1990s. Also critical to the story are the venture capitalists who clustered in the area. In addition, the tech sector became a darling of Washington, winning favorable tax treatment for things like stock options and capital gains. It was also lightly regulated. A young Steve Jobs, growing up in an area full of engineers, launched Apple from his garage in Los Altos. The personal computer revolution led to the internet revolution and e-commerce. The hot product became software, not hardware. Jobs, in a second act, revolutionized mobile phones. Then came the rise of Google (internet search) and Facebook (social media). Tesla, starting from its perch in Palo Alto, hoped to drag the world into an age of electric cars. For years now, cities across America have been asking: How do we become a tech hub like Silicon Valley? Good things, however, don't often last forever. Though the Valley's tech champions have grown even more wealthy and influential during the pandemic, Washington's attitude toward the sector is quickly souring. Immigration became more restrictive during the Trump years. Tech firms are increasingly criticized for non-inclusive hiring practices. Some like Oracle and Tesla are leaving for lower-tax places. Housing is so expensive that public servants like teachers and police officers can barely afford to live there. In fact, Silicon Valley doesn't even produce silicon chips anymore—that's been outsourced to other places, from Arizona to Asia. As it says on the back of every iPhone: "Designed by Apple in California. Assembled in China."

(5)

PHILADELPHIA, PENNSYLVANIA

February 2021

Philadelphia, at the time of the American Revolution, was arguably North America's most important city. It became, after all, the first capital of the new United States. Thereafter, it quickly became the young country's most important manufacturing center. The population almost doubled from 1820 to 1840, boosted by arrivals from the surrounding hinterland, alongside immigrants from places like Ireland and Germany. Black Americans were about a tenth of the city's people, according to Alasdair Roberts in his book "America's First Great Depression." New York became the largest U.S. city by total population around 1810, pushing Philadelphia to the number two spot. Developments like Andrew Jackson's closure of the Philadelphia-based Second Bank of the United States—plus the opening of the Erie Canal—gave New York an upper hand in finance that it would never relinquish. Still, Philadelphia would remain America's number two city until Chicago passed it in 1900. Throughout the 20th century, the City of Brotherly Love remained a place of great influence, with lots of people and lots of commerce. But the era of deindustrialization that began around the 1970s hit like a thunderbolt. Today, Philadelphia ranks just eighth among U.S. metro areas, with just over

6m people (it ranked fifth as recently as 2010). It might soon fall to ninth as Atlanta adds people at a faster clip. More importantly and regrettably, the *city* of Philadelphia itself has one of the highest poverty rates of any big U.S. city. Pew Research, last April, estimated the rate to be nearly 25%, highest among the country's ten largest cities. Pew also shows the city ranking below national average for small businesses per capita, college graduates per capita, median incomes, rates of preschool enrollment and labor participation rates. Just 14% of the city's people are foreign born, compared to Houston's 28%, Boston's 27% or Chicago's 20%. One shortcoming is that it doesn't have quite the same appeal to millennials and tourists as other northeastern cities like New York, Boston and Washington. One manifestation of this: Just four non-North American airlines flew to Philadelphia in 2019 (British Airways, its Irish subsidiary Aer Lingus, Germany's Lufthansa and Qatar Airways). More than 20 flew to Boston. The city continues to have fiscal pressures as well, long after nearly filing for bankruptcy in the early 1990s. Former mayor Michael Nutter, speaking with Wharton Business Daily last week, said 65% of the city's budget is for personnel, implying difficulties containing costs without job cuts, wage cuts, or cuts to health and pension benefits. In December, the city's budget office, grappling with the Covid crisis, wrote: "Budget balancing actions, like revenue increases and spending reductions, are highly likely to be necessary in [fiscal year 2022] and beyond." A spike in violent crime isn't helping. A bleak picture? The city's problems are challenging for sure. But things do look brighter when considering the entire metro area, where key indicators like wealth, poverty and education compare favorably to national averages. The city itself has many bright spots too, including world-class education and health facilities, with all the high-paying jobs those sectors bring. Pew's Larry Eichel says 12 of the city's top 15 employers are either education or medical related. The other three are Comcast (the big cable company that also owns NBCUniversal), Texas-based American Airlines (which operates a large hub at Philadelphia airport) and Allied Universal (a provider of security guards). Other notable Philadelphia firms include the food service giant Aramark and can manufacturer Crown Holdings. In the wealthy western suburbs are corporate titans like AmerisourceBergen (pharma distribution) and Vanguard (financial services).

NORTH DAKOTA

March 2021

For much of America, the last recession before Covid came in 2008 and 2009, when housing prices collapsed nationwide. Not so for North Dakota, which exhibited its own unique economic trajectory during the 2010s. During the first half of the decade, it was among the fastest-growing economies—in the *world*. With oil prices topping $100 per barrel for three straight years, western parts of the state enjoying the horizontal drilling boom—the town of Williston, for example—couldn't build homes, roads, hotels, eateries and medical facilities fast enough. Americans with little education could land oil jobs at companies like Haliburton that paid six-figure salaries. In 2012, the number of airline seats departing Williston airport jumped by 42%, according to the aviation data provider Cirium. The next year, seats doubled. The boom led North Dakota's economy to grow a stunning 25% in 2012, followed by 4% growth in 2013 and 9% growth in 2014, St. Louis Fed statistics show. Wow. But it all came crashing down when oil prices collapsed in late 2014. Boom became bust. Just as growth in the national economy was picking up, North Dakota's GDP contracted 6% and then 8%, in 2015 and 2016, respectively. State GDP remains smaller today than it was at its 2014 peak. And that was true in 2019 as well, before Covid started. In 2016, Williston's airline capacity plummeted nearly 40%. The western North Dakota oil roller coaster, however, masks a much sunnier situation to the east. There, unemployment stands at just 3% today, according to Jeremy Jackson of North Dakota State University. In Williams County, by contrast, where Williston is located, the unemployment rate is 10%. Agriculture is one important sector for the state, with farms growing products like corn, wheat, soy, barley and sugar beets. Prices for many of these crops are helpfully rising in 2021. In the tech space, Microsoft has one of its largest campuses in Fargo, the state's largest metro area. Ag tech—applying new technologies to farming—is a hot area. So is drone research around Grand Forks and its Air Force base, with its empty airspace and open land. Last week, Jackson's Center for Public Choice and Private Enterprise published its latest monthly update on the state's economy, noting a growing labor force, rising wages and higher tax collections. The report also shows that "North Dakota's current economic path is relatively independent of trends in the price of crude oil." That said, times are still tough in places like Williston—its latest blow was the cancellation of the Keystone Pipeline, which would have brought crude from North Dakota's Bakken region to Gulf refineries in Texas and Louisiana. That said, Bakken crude is already flowing through the Dakota Access pipeline.

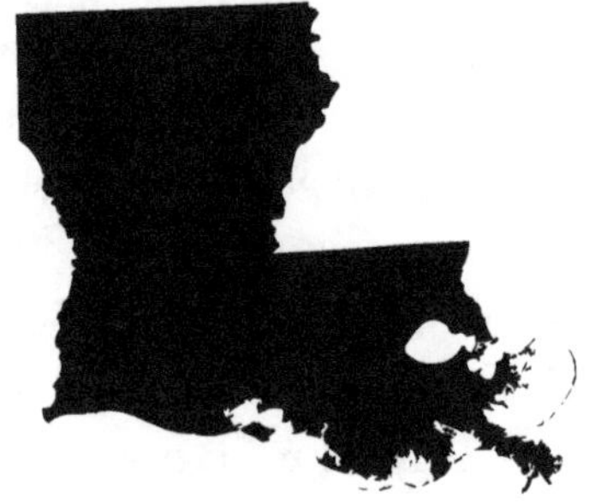

NEW ORLEANS, LOUISIANA

March 2021

On March 17 of last year, just as Covid was forcing businesses across the U.S. to close, the Brookings Institution gave its best guess on which major cities would be hit hardest. Las Vegas and Orlando ranked most vulnerable, unsurprisingly given their exposure to tourism. Next on the list? New Orleans, a city likewise a magnet for visitors but also one greatly exposed to Louisiana's large energy sector. Unfortunately, Brookings was right. The Covid crisis has indeed proved extremely difficult for the Crescent City, already deeply challenged going into the crisis. Unlike Las Vegas, Orlando and many other cities across the sunbelt, New Orleans never did experience a population boom. On the contrary, the city started losing population as early as the 1960s. In 2005, Hurricane Katrina devastated the area—Katrina still stands today as the costliest natural disaster in U.S. history; it killed 1,800 people and left some 100,000 homeless. Large numbers then left the city, many migrating to nearby Houston, contributing to a boom there. It was another big blow to an economy that was once the largest and economically most important city in the U.S. South, boosted by its strategic position at the mouth of the mighty Mississippi. But its importance would peak just before the Civil War, when it was a center of the cotton trade, which was no less important in *that* era, than the oil trade is today. The cotton trade, of course, was underpinned by slavery, abolished after the war. Like elsewhere in the South, New Orleans—for a full century— would choose continued subjugation rather than integration when it came to its Black population. African Americans, striving to overcome that legacy, account for about 60% of the city's population today. For the New Orleans metro area as a whole, the total population is back to roughly where it was pre-Katrina—about 1.3m people in 2019. That ranks it just 54th among all U.S. metros in size, just behind Richmond and just ahead of Louisville. It's also one of America's poorest big cities, highlighted by its 26% pre-Covid poverty rate. Crime and corruption, real or perceived, are major deterrents to development. The racial gap is still a problem too, with 71% of African American families earning below a living wage, according to Lamar Gardare of Data Center— the figure is just 31% for the city's Whites. Carmen James Randolph of the Greater New Orleans Foundation pins the current unemployment rate of the city's Black males at 47%. Available and affordable transportation and childcare remain key obstacles. Overall, the Covid crisis initially caused total unemployment to spike higher than it reached even after Katrina. It doesn't help that cities built on river shipping—think Buffalo, Cincinnati and St. Louis as well—are disadvantaged in today's world of railways, highways and airways. But all is not lost. Far from it. In some ways, the New Orleans economy now appears excellently positioned to emerge from the Covid pandemic. Tourism, energy and petrochemicals are already coming back, and New Orleans tourism isn't so dependent on *foreign visitors.* Michael Hecht, who heads the economic development nonprofit Greater New Orleans, describes rising hotel occupancy rates, more airport traffic, signs of a rebound in business conventions and lots of live events scheduled for the fall. New Orleans never experienced the housing boom and bust of the 2000s. But, Hecht explains, it is enjoying the current strength in housing markets, boosted by migrants from bigger cities and remote workers moving at least part-time to places of sun, leisure and low housing costs. Pre-Covid, New Orleans had one of the fastest-growing immigrant populations. It has a brand-new airport terminal. It plans a $1.5b expansion of its seaport as well, to make it more competitive with Houston in the currently booming world of container shipping. The city has a major NASA assembly plant at a time when space commerce is hot and Washington plans the creation of a new Space Force. Hecht points to cost and workforce diversity advantages for tech companies. Tulane University, building on its expertise in tropical viruses like Yellow Fever, is playing an important role in Covid research. And perhaps most interestingly, New Orleans has a wealth of expertise in managing the effects of climate change—expertise that it's now selling to the world. America's Netherlands? Like its Dutch counterpart, New Orleans is among the world's most ecologically fragile places, with areas actually *below* sea level. New Orleans though, would argue that it has the better food.

One more point to make about New Orleans, from Quentin L. Messer Jr., chief of the New Orleans Business Alliance. He notes the city's insufficient supply of capital to fund entrepreneurs and small businesses. One reason for this shortage, he argues, is that New Orleans never had any big companies go public. In Austin, where the tech economy is now booming, large numbers of millionaires were created from Dell's IPO in the 1980s. Silicon Valley in California of course has a similar abundance of people made wealthy by IPOs, who in turn often invest that money into their own or other local businesses.

NASHVILLE, TENNESSEE

March 2021

J ust before the Covid crisis started, the Wall Street Journal published a list of its hottest U.S. job markets. Austin was number one. And number two? That distinction went to Nashville, the state capital of Tennessee. Why? Look at the city's booming tech sector. In 2019, Amazon—the biggest U.S. tech employer of all—announced the creation of 5,000 new downtown jobs. The company today counts Nashville as one of its three main corporate offices along with Seattle and Arlington (Virginia). In 2015, Lyft, the ride-hailing company, put its customer service center in Nashville. Postmates and Eventbrite are two other west coast tech companies that moved part of their operations there. Importantly, a number of smaller homegrown tech companies have sold themselves or gone public, creating a reserve of new capital for local reinvestment. From 2014 to 2019, according to the Greater Nashville Technology Council (GNTC), the area saw a 36% increase in tech jobs—growth for the U.S. as a whole was just 23%. Overall, the metro area population is now approaching 2m, having grown a bullish 17% in the 2010s. That makes it similar in size to Austin and Silicon Valley. Affordability is clearly a draw, with no state income tax and housing prices still about 3% below the national average. So says the GNTC, which also claims that Nashville is the third largest college town in the nation, with more than 120,000 students attending 20 different universities. Vanderbilt, the most prominent, is the area's largest employer. That includes the university's medical center, an anchor of the region's giant health care sector. Also headquartered in Nashville: HCA, one of America's largest hospital chains. It was this $90b health care sector, in fact, that helped Nashville avoid the worst of the 2008-09 recession. The Covid crisis, however, devastated what's by most counts the city's second-largest industry: tourism. More than 16m visitors came in 2019, many lured by Nashville's status as the epicenter of country music—"Music City USA." The Opryland resort and convention center calls itself the largest non-gaming hotel property in the country—2,888 rooms and more than 700,000 square feet of meeting space. As it waits for tourism to revive, Nashville has other enviable advantages, aside from tech, education, and health care. Being the state capital helps. Finance companies—AllianceBernstein is a notable example—are joining tech firms in moving all or part of their operations to Nashville. Other firms headquartered in the area include Dollar General, the Randstad staffing agency and the restaurant chains Shoney's and Cracker Barrel. And critically, Nashville is a top beneficiary of the auto sector's shift southward away from Detroit and the Midwest, spearheaded by foreign manufacturers. As early as 1983, Japan's Toyota established a $7b car factory just outside of Nashville, currently employing about 7,000 workers. It now has a separate engine factory nearby as well. Bridgestone, the Japanese tire-maker, likewise has its U.S. headquarters in the area. It's a far cry from the city's earliest days when it was considered the far western part of the U.S., ripe for land speculation. Those were the days of President Andrew Jackson, the city's most famous politician. Limestone was a big part of the economy then, as was shipping along the Cumberland River. As historian Carole Bucy describes, it later became the site of a DuPont plant employing 50,000 workers. Today, in addition to all the new industries moving in, so too are many retirees, attracted by the mild weather, affordable living, good health care and proximity to attractions like the Great Smoky Mountains. Some are so-called "halfbacks" who originally migrated southward from places like New York to Florida but are now moving northward to areas like Tennessee and North Carolina. Nashville does of course have its challenges, including housing costs that are sure enough starting to rise rapidly. A major flood in 2010 was extremely costly. A damaging tornado hit the city just as the pandemic was starting last spring. On Christmas Day last year, a bomb downtown caused injuries and major property damage. Nashville, meanwhile, doesn't yet have quite the international stature as America's Big-League cities, notes Amr El-Husseini, head of the Lodestone Advisory Group. A new nonstop British Airways flight to London helps. But that's the only international offering aside from those to Canada and Mexico. El-Husseini, meanwhile, cautions about offering generous government incentives to companies creating mere back-office jobs that might be automated away in the coming decade. It's important, he says, for Nashville to also invest in entrepreneurs creating growth companies. In one sense, the region's governance model is helpful: Unlike St. Louis for example, Nashville and its surrounding county pioneered consolidated metro area governance in the 1960s. That enables decisions optimized for the metro area as a whole. Finally, here's a thought from Nashville's former mayor Karl Dean, who says the city has the "Three T's" essential to a successful economy in the 2020s: Talent, technology and tolerance.

(9)

JUNEAU, ALASKA

March 2021

With fewer people than all but two other states, it's not often that Alaska makes national news. Last week, however, it played host to a closely watched diplomatic meeting between the U.S. and China. The meeting was in Anchorage, the state's largest city. Anchorage is *not* the state's capital though. The state's capital is Juneau, a city—actually more of a town—with just 32,000 people. Of the 210 U.S. media markets ranked by Neilson, Juneau comes in at number 207. But it's not just a small place, with all the economic challenges associated with smallness. It's also geographically remote—a 20-hour drive to Anchorage; a roughly 40-hour drive to Vancouver or Seattle. Better take an Alaska Airlines flight instead. So how do the residents of Juneau earn a living? Naturally, being the state capital, government work is the leading profession, and a leading reason why Juneau's unemployment rates are typically lower than the state and national averages. But as Brian Holst points out, Juneau has been losing government jobs all decade, in part because technology has allowed dispersion of some administration work to other areas of the state. Holst is the Executive Director of the Juneau Economic Development Council, whose latest report on economic indicators shows government jobs accounting for a full 45% of all local earnings from wages and salaries in 2019. It also incidentally shows Juneau's population declining between 2012 and 2019. If close to half of the economy is government, what private sector activities make up the other half? Fortunately, during normal times—but unfortunately during the pandemic—Juneau is a major tourist attraction, welcoming 1.3m cruise passengers in 2019. In 2020, alas, it saw just one small ship carrying 36 people. Without the tourists last year, the normal influx of summer-season workers didn't come either. And it's still unclear when the cruise sector will get started again. Tourism, by the way, normally accounts for 20% of Juneau's sales tax receipts. In so many American places big and small, health care is a major employer. But that's less the case in southeast Alaska. The state's large military bases are in Anchorage and Fairbanks, not Juneau. The oil industry, which dominates the statewide economy (roughly half of its GDP), resides in the far north. The area around Juneau, however, does have two of the state's five largest mines, thriving at the moment with many mineral prices rising. Mining jobs (unlike tourism jobs) also tend to pay well. Hecla Mining, most importantly, owns one of the world's largest silver mines on nearby Admiralty Island. Couer Mining controls a nearby mine featuring gold, the chief reason many people rushed to Alaska in the first place during the 1890s. Another notable sector for Juneau: transportation, including the helicopter firms that cater to tourists. And then there are the marine-focused industries owing to Juneau's unique geography. It has its share of the state's giant seafood industry (Alaska produces more seafood than all other states combined). At the moment, Juneau's housing industry is very strong, mirroring national trends. But also like other places in the U.S., affordable housing is a problem. Officials in fact would like to attract remote workers from places like California and Seattle. But it's a costly place to live. Another deterrent is problematic internet speed and reliability. Holst of the Economic Development Council did say salmon fisheries are recovering as restaurants reopen. He's optimistic that cruise traffic will return before long. And cannabis has become a niche growth sector.

PUERTO RICO

March 2021

S poiler alert: It's not a happy story. But before going any further, let's be clear about Puerto Rico's political status. It's not a state, but rather one of five U.S. "territories" that elect their own governors and legislatures but don't cast votes for president (the other four permanently inhabited territories are Guam, the U.S. Virgin Islands, American Samoa and the Northern Mariana Islands). Puerto Rico's 3.2m people—there were 3.8m as recently as 2014—are U.S. citizens, meaning they can live and work anywhere in the country without any special documentation. They can and often do serve in the U.S. military. But they lack full voting representation not just in presidential elections but also in Congress. They typically don't pay federal taxes on income earned on the island. But nor do they have the same eligibility for some federal programs. That's been the story more or less since 1900, when Congress established a civilian government for Puerto Rico, after taking possession of the Caribbean island in a war with Spain. Early on, its big industry was sugar. It later became a place of geopolitical significance during the Cold War when its rather strong economic growth was held up as a Caribbean counterexample to communist Cuba. As the economist Jose Villamil recounted in a 2014 lecture, Puerto Rico in the 1960s and '70s began to lose some foreign investment in low-wage sectors (i.e., shoe manufacturing) to new competitors including Spain. But it also became a center of petrochemicals, pharmaceuticals and medical devices. Not until the mid-1970s did Puerto Rico experience its first recession. Uncomfortably, much of its investment from the U.S. mainland was thanks to generous tax incentives, for research and development, for example, and the right to return profits back to the mainland tax free. Congress, alas, ended Section 936 of the tax code in 1996, thus phasing out these lucrative benefits over a ten-year period. That brings the story to 2006 when the housing bubble was inflating across the U.S., Puerto Rico included. The pop, when it came, hit hard. While the rest of the U.S. recovered, however, Puerto Rico never did. The 2010s would be a lost decade economically, scarred by fiscal ruin and brutal natural disasters. In 2016, Congress enacted a board to oversee Puerto Rico's finances and conduct a bankruptcy-like restructuring of its huge debts; Washington did not however provide any taxpayer bailouts. Hurricane Maria obliterated much of the island's economy in 2017. Earthquakes followed in 2019. Then Covid last year, which shrank GDP by about 8%. According to a Congressional analysis, the island suffers from low labor participation rates, high rates of outmigration (notably to the Orlando area of Florida), intensified global competition and a declining birth rate. The San Juan metro area alone saw its population shrink by 14% in the 2010s. Census data show 92% of Puerto Rico's households earn less than $75,000 annually (the percentage is just 66% in Florida). A full 45% of residents live below the poverty line (15% in Florida). Per capita income, says former Congressman Luis Gutierrez, is half what it is in the poorest U.S. state Mississippi. Crime, including drug trafficking given its strategic location, is a concern. Villamil, when he spoke in the early 2010s, estimated that federal transfers accounted for more than a fifth of average incomes. After a decade-long recession, what's the path forward? Tourism, for sure, as the sector recovers from the Covid shock (San Juan is a major cruise port, with an airport owned and run by a Mexican operator). The island still has an active biopharma industry—Amgen for one employs about 3,000 people there. Jorge Martel of T-Mobile explains how Puerto Rico, after much of its telecom infrastructure was damaged by the hurricanes, is building back with leading-edge 5G cellular technology, making it a leader in 5G rollouts. The island's bondholders have agreed to cut their claims from $19b to just over $7b, according to the financial oversight board's executive director Natalie A. Jaresko (fast fact: she was once Ukraine's finance minister). She hopes Puerto Rico can exit bankruptcy before the year's end. Some islanders want statehood, though that's a tall task politically given the national implications for Senate power and Presidential votes (it would help Democrats over Republicans). Helpfully, the $1.9 trillion American Rescue Plan makes households in Puerto Rico fully eligible for child tax credits for the first time. But there's a long way to go, especially in areas like power infrastructure and poverty alleviation. The oversight board recently revised its GNP forecasts upward thanks largely to the $14b-plus in aid to be received from the three big federal stimulus packages. But it still sees the economy shrinking 4% in the year to June, barely growing at all next year, and then shrinking again during the two subsequent years.

(11)

DENVER, COLORADO

April 2021

The Covid catastrophe hit every city in America last year. No exceptions. But on a shortlist of places that held up surprisingly well, Denver ranks high. A mile high. Like many of America's western cities, people first came to Denver for natural resources, in this case gold just before the Civil War. It evolved from more than just a mining encampment with big help from the railroads. It eventually was chosen as capital of Colorado, which became a state in 1876. Another boost came during World War II and the Cold War that followed, when the federal government chose to place many of its strategic bases, labs and other facilities in the hard-to-reach mountains, far from the coasts (much like Russia placed much of its strategic post WWII aerospace facilities as far away from Germany as possible). Nevertheless, Denver remained a natural resource dependent economy as late as the 1980s. It was oil and gas that dominated then. But the '80s energy bust was a wake-up call. Like Houston, Denver entered the 1990s with economic diversification a top priority. Its efforts by any measure worked, leading to today's multi-industry success. To be sure, natural resources remain critical. Weld County, a large expanse of land north of metro Denver, produces energy, yes, but is also an agricultural powerhouse, specializing in livestock. Naturally, as the state capital, Denver counts government as an important sector. But not just state government. Denver also has one of the highest concentrations of *federal* government jobs outside of Washington. Uncle Sam's presence includes big offices of agencies like the Department of the Interior. Federal labs conduct research in areas like renewable energy. Then there's the military, including the U.S. Air Force Academy in nearby Colorado Springs, technically a separate metro area from Denver but with plenty of close ties. As with most thriving cities at the dawn of the 2020s, "eds and meds" provide a backbone of well-compensated employment. Boulder is home to the University of Colorado. And while Denver isn't as heavy on medical jobs as say, Nashville or Philadelphia, institutions like the Centura hospital network certainly have a big role in the labor market. DaVita, which operates a nationwide network of kidney dialysis centers, is a notable private-sector health giant (it generated $11b in revenues during 2019). But that's only just scratching the surface. Denver has long been a center of the cable television industry. It's home to many aerospace firms, including some working on a new generation of supersonic planes. It's also home to many breweries, from mom-and-pop craft operations to Molson Coors, America's second-largest brewer after Anheuser Busch. And Anheuser isn't even headquartered in America anymore (it's owned by a Belgian firm). Then again, Molson Coors isn't headquartered in Denver anymore—it moved to Chicago—but it retains a large Mile High presence. Enough about beer. There's also Arrow Electronics, Dish Networks, Western Union, Liberty Media, VF Apparel… all are Fortune 500 companies headquartered in Denver. That said, it's not quite in the big leagues when it comes to corporate headquarters. In that category, it's no Dallas-Fort Worth, let alone New York City, Chicago or the San Francisco Bay Area. But Denver remains a much smaller metro area, ranking just 19th in the country with its roughly 2m people. For sure though, companies based in places like the San Francisco Bay Area are adding jobs in Denver, sometimes employing more there than at headquarters. Salesforce and Strava are two Bay Area firms with a big Denver presence. Palantir, which uses Big Data to help clients like the Pentagon, did in fact move its HQ from Silicon Valley to Denver. It's not just a California exodus thing, however. People and companies are coming from both east and west, often attracted by the outdoors/mountain lifestyle. Firms undoubtedly like Denver's large pool of college-educated workers, including many software engineers. J.J. Ament, who runs the privately funded Metro Denver Economic Development Corporation, clearly has a lot to work with as he tries to lure employers to the area—the lifestyle, the education, the skills, the sunny weather, the nearby ski slopes, expanding public transport, a vibrant downtown… And one more powerful appeal: The city's airport. This quarter, Denver has more scheduled domestic airline seats than any other U.S. airport except Atlanta. It's a rare airport with not one, not two, but three airline hubs—United, Southwest and Frontier Airlines all connect traffic there. With long driving distances from most other cities, Denver has always punched above its weight in terms of air traffic. Its stature only grew during the pandemic, when airlines cut nonstop flights and funneled more of their traffic through mid-continent hubs. It was an awful 2020 for sure, with traffic falling 51% from the year prior. But most other hubs saw much bigger declines. One reason for Denver's relative success: Its appeal to tourists and remote workers looking for outdoor open spaces. Ament, interestingly, says it was already first in the nation for remote working *before* the pandemic. Make no mistake, the hit to Denver's large tourism sector was severe; Ament estimates that about half of current Denver-area unemployment is tied to tourism and hospitality. Even as tourism and convention business returns, the Mile High City will still face familiar problems like increasingly expensive housing prices—better than California for sure, but not as cheap as Texas. It doesn't yet pack the global punch of a mega-city; the airport's menu of intercontinental nonstops includes just a few flights to Europe and Japan. The Covid crisis, furthermore, did slow what had been rapid population growth. But never mind the setbacks. As economies go, Denver has reached the mountaintop.

(12)

LEWISTON, MAINE

April 2021

They came across the border in droves. Many couldn't speak English. On *their* side of the border: job opportunities few and far between. On the other: A booming economy that couldn't find workers fast enough. No, we're not talking about the U.S. border with Mexico. We're talking about the U.S. border with Canada, across which some 1m French-speaking migrants came during the 19th and 20th centuries. They came to fast-growing industrial New England cities like Lewiston, Maine, no less vibrant a textile hub then, than Silicon Valley or Austin are vibrant tech hubs today. Unfortunately for Lewiston, textile manufacturing no longer sits at the center of America's industrial economy. Those days have long passed. Most of the clothes Americans wear today are imported from lower-wage countries, something true for many decades now. New England's larger coastal cities, led by Boston, have reinvented themselves. Portland, Maine's largest city, is a vibrant tourist destination during summers. It's also famous for its lobsters. That said, Maine as a whole, which is almost as large as Indiana in land area, is one of the slowest-growing states nationwide, with its population up by just 75% in the past 100 years. Most states have at least doubled, and some much more than that; hardly a jobs magnet for millennials. Maine is also the second oldest state after Florida, with 19% of its people over the age of 65. Lewiston itself is a microcosm of such trends—its population of about 40,000 shrank by about 1% during the 2010s. Per capita income is about $25k, compared to $37k in Portland and $45k in Boston. Like in so many communities across America, a central pillar of Lewiston's economy is health care, responsible for about one in five jobs, according to Lincoln Jeffers, who runs Lewiston's economic and community development department. Also important is the education sector, including Bates College. The city, Maine's second largest, isn't much of a tourist draw like Portland, Kennebunkport and other coastal cities, though it does have some attractions like a popular balloon festival. It's not the state capital—that's Augusta. Walmart does have a distribution center in Lewiston. The clothing retailer L.L. Bean, based in nearby Freeport, is a sizeable employer. And yes, the city does have some high-tech manufacturing including Elmet Technologies, which works with minerals used in things like airplanes, semiconductors and medical equipment. The city has tried for years to secure a passenger rail link to Portland, which would facilitate commuting to a job there. Rail links to Boston and Montreal would help too, and President Biden's enthusiasm for rail investment offers some hope. Lewiston is separately trying to lure businesses to its historic downtown. It's still home to one of the largest French-speaking communities in the U.S., according to Bates College professor Mary Rice-DeFosse. Most interestingly, it's today an epicenter of migration from fast-growing Africa, including francophone countries like the Democratic Republic of Congo. But the majority are refugees from Somalia. A typical pattern, Jeffers explains, involves Somalis first migrating to bigger cities, most importantly Minneapolis and Atlanta. But at some point, word got out that Maine offered a safer environment and better schools. Portland was a major draw but soaring housing costs there have made Lewiston an attractive alternative. As a city that's 87% White, the arrival of so many Africans has indeed led to some tensions. But leading political figures of Lewiston and Maine more broadly have hammered home the need for more people—shrinking populations make it extremely difficult to achieve economic growth. Within Maine itself, rural residents have come to larger cities as the state's paper mills have closed or contracted. Others have come to retire, lured by a low cost of living and good health care. As for the Covid crisis, it devastated employment in the restaurant and retail sectors. But most establishments survived with help from government aid, and most are now starting to see business return. Says Jeffers about Lewiston this spring: "Everybody I know is as busy as can be."

THE CHEYENNE RIVER INDIAN RESERVATION, SOUTH DAKOTA

April 2021

Technically speaking, Wheeler County, in rural Georgia, is the poorest place in America. But only because its large prison population brings down average incomes. The true poverty capital of America is central South Dakota, home of the Cheyenne River Indian Reservation. Ziebach County, which covers the western part of the reservation, had a per capita personal income of just $19,940 in 2019, according to the U.S. Bureau of Economic Analysis. By comparison, South Dakota's *statewide* per capita income is about $57,000, while that of the U.S. as a whole is roughly $60,000. Nearly half of residents live below the poverty line. Socioeconomic problems prevalent throughout large swathes of the U.S., including substandard education and healthcare, are of grave concern here. So is inadequate housing, alcoholism, drug abuse and suicide. The reservation, in other words, is a disturbing symbol of the economic inequality found across the U.S.—but in extreme form. At a time when the national unemployment rate has fallen below 7%, joblessness on the reservation exceeds 60%, according to Remi

Bald Eagle, the intergovernmental affairs coordinator for the Cheyenne River Sioux Tribe. Few jobs exist outside the government sector, which includes both the tribal government and the federal government. Federal involvement is mostly the responsibility of the Bureau of Indian Affairs in Washington (part of the Department of Interior) and the Indian Health Service (part of the Department of Health and Human Services). In a typical arrangement, the Feds will contract out public service work to the tribal government, to handle law enforcement, for example. The U.S government hospital in Eagle Butte, the reservation's main town with about 1,000 people, is one of the largest employers. The tribe also earns some revenue leasing land to the beef industry. A few tourists pass through the vast reservation during summers, notably on route to the Sturgis Motorcycle Rally (Sturgis is in the far western part of South Dakota, near Mount Rushmore). Some outsiders come to use tribal lands for hunting as well. But the reservation's tourism revenues are negligible. And the land contains no meaningful quantities of natural resources like oil; the Indian Wars of the 19th century, after all, were largely about evicting tribes from resource-rich lands, through a combination of genocide and forced relocation. To the reservation's south is Wounded Knee, site of an infamous 1890 massacre of Lakota Sioux people. But the main feature of the reservation's economy today is not what's near but what's far. Everything, seemingly, is far in these isolated parts. Interstate-90, the nearest major road, is some 100 miles away from Eagle Butte. Sioux Falls, a thriving city, is a five-hour drive. The reservation itself, Remy Bad Eagle says, has just four paved roads. The lone school was built in the 1950s. The tribe does operate the oldest Native-American-owned telecom company in the U.S., with modern fiber optic-speed internet. The problem is that most people there can't afford it. So at a time when broadband access is increasingly critical to participating in the economy, fewer than 60% of the reservation's households have high-speed access, according to Census figures, and more than 30% don't even have a computer. There's hope that President Biden's infrastructure proposal will lead to some improvements. It features multiple mentions of Indian tribal areas.

(1 4)

ATLANTA, GEORGIA

April 2021

And you thought Florida was a hotly contested political battleground? These days, the hinge of national political power is just to the north, in Georgia. Votes there helped put President Biden into office. Votes there—even more dramatically—put Democrats in control of the Senate. With the stakes so high, no wonder why Georgia and its elections are again at the center of national attention. This time, it's a new state voting law that critics see as a manifestation of reawakening demons—demons of racial injustice. Caught in the vortex of the dispute is the economy of Atlanta, Georgia's capital and—some like to say—the capital of the American South. Make that the "New South," as promoters call it, distinct from the old South and its troubled past. Atlanta, said one its mayors famously, was too busy to hate. To be sure, Atlanta has had its share of racial tensions, as Frederick Allen makes clear in his 1996 book "Atlanta Rising." Another book, by Kevin Kruse—White Flight: Atlanta and the Making of Modern Conservatism— offers another look at the city's complicated racial history. This year, the city lost its chance to host baseball All-Star Game, after the sport deemed Georgia's new voting law unacceptable. But will the economy suffer? Probably not much. Atlanta's economic fortunes rest on firm ground in 21st century America, in one respect for the same reason it was so important to the South in the 19th century. The city started life as a national transportation hub, for railroads. Now, it's a global transportation hub, for airlines. Covid-skewed trends in 2020 aside, Atlanta's airport handles more passengers than any other worldwide, thanks in part to the strength and reach of Delta Air Lines, one of several corporate giants based in "A-Town." Another is UPS, a cargo giant. The most famous is Coca-Cola, an Atlanta institution since the late 1800s. There's Home Depot, currently thriving amid the home-centric spending boom. There's the cable company Cox Communications. You can include CNN too, though it's technically now part of AT&T, a Dallas-Fort Worth-based company. Atlanta's aviation prominence is nothing new. As early as 1930, it was the third busiest airport in the nation behind only New York and Chicago (these cities remain larger aviation markets today, but traffic is split across multiple airports). World War II was a major moment for the economy, as the city became a key production site for aerial bombers and the military supply center for the entire southeast. After the war, manufacturers like Ford and Lockheed established manufacturing plants, often employing a racially mixed workforce. Atlanta would gain national prominence over subsequent decades, with the rise of figures like Martin Luther King Jr. and Jimmy Carter. The 1980s was a breakout decade, ushering in the great sunbelt migration that continues today. Atlanta entered the *global* spotlight by hosting the Olympics in 1996. During the 2010s, its population grew 14%, boosted by many African American decedents of the great northern migration returning south. It's still the city with the largest percentage of African American business owners, according to several studies, as well as millionaires and middle-class households. Today, Atlanta is the country's ninth largest metro area with about 6m people, just behind Philadelphia. The area's second largest employer after Delta is Emory University and its health center. With air travel coming back and the economy more generally reopening, metro Atlanta's unemployment rate fell to 4.1% in March; that's well below the 6% national average. One thing Atlanta is *not*, which proved a blessing in disguise during the pandemic, is a big tourist attraction. In fact, much of Atlanta's abundant airport traffic is merely connecting there, en route to Florida or some other destination. Fewer than ten foreign airlines flew to Atlanta from overseas in 2019, and most of those only because of close business ties to Delta. Atlanta, incidentally, did lose some of its banking clout to nearby Charlotte (the latest loss was SunTrust, now called Truist). Looking ahead, Korea's SK Innovation is building a $2.6b battery plant just outside the metro area. It won't be Atlanta's only connection to the auto industry—several foreign car builders have their U.S. bases there, including Germany's Mercedes and Porsche. There are plenty of technology firms too, many on the front lines of wireless communication developments like the Internet of Things.

(15)

DELAWARE

May 2021

They call it the "First State" for a reason. Delaware was the first of America's original 13 colonies to ratify the U.S. Constitution in 1787. Going even farther back, its largest city Wilmington started as a Swedish colony in the 1600s. But fast forward to 2021, and Americans are becoming acquainted with the First State for another reason. It's the home state of the current U.S. President Joe Biden. Biden's election, sure enough, made Wilmington a busy place this winter, serving as the headquarters of his presidential transition. Incidentally, this helped struggling local hotels, shops and restaurants hurt by the Covid crisis. It helped the city's convention center as well. But Biden works from Washington now, and Wilmington is back to being what it's always been: A niche financial hub. Well, maybe not always. Delaware's rise as a banking haven began in the 1980s, as deregulation swept through the industry. In 1980, South Dakota pioneered an end to laws capping interest rates, prompting Citicorp for one to establish a big presence there (which remains today). Delaware followed with its own state laws to attract banks, adopting what it called its "Luxembourg" strategy. The Federal Reserve chief at the time, Paul Volcker, wasn't happy.

A 1983 Washington Post article quoted him thus: "I am seriously concerned about the possibility of widely divergent and inconsistent laws governing both banks and thrift powers, with deposit-taking organizations shopping for the most permissive rules, and states competing to pass such laws in order to enhance local employment." Delaware got its way though, and quickly became a hub for credit card lending most importantly. JPMorgan Chase has its credit card division in Wilmington. So does the British bank Barclays, which purchased the Delaware lender Juniper in 2004. Bank of America acquired Wilmington's MBNA in 2006. And so on. According to Delaware Prosperity Partnership, the state's economic development agency, Goldman Sachs—a recent convert to consumer lending—will add up to 150 new jobs on Wilmington's waterfront. Barclays is adding hundreds of jobs as well. Overall, finance, including lots of activity in areas like student loans and insurance, accounts for nearly 10% of the state's jobs, more than any other sector. Delaware, however, is more than just a haven for credit card lenders. It's more broadly a haven for all of Corporate America, offering business-friendly courts, flexible rules on corporate governance and favorable tax laws. Believe it or not, nearly 70% of America's Fortune 500 companies are legally incorporated in Delaware. And a third of the state government's revenue comes from fees these companies pay. Even more controversially, Delaware's corporate friendly rules extend to privacy—there's often no need to disclose the names of people associated with a newly-formed business. As a result, Delaware is often accused of facilitating tax avoidance and even illicit activities. Historically, Delaware followed a similar path to other northeastern cities, growing wealthy with industry but struggling as industry moved to lower-cost places starting around the 1970s. For many years, the state's most important company by far was Dupont, a chemical firm which produces a diverse array of things like semiconductors, printer ink, dietary supplements and water purifiers. But as a recent Wall Street Journal report explained, years of downsizing and a giant merger with Dow Chemical led to nearly 10,000 lost jobs in the state of Delaware. Today, the Journal wrote, Dupont is Delaware's twelfth largest employer, down from number one 20 years ago. Consistent with much of the modern-day American economy, the state's largest employer is now a health care network. JP Morgan is number two. Other big employers include the Dover Air Force base and the University of Delaware. Poultry farming is a major industry. A Delaware Business Times report last month highlighted the scarcity of land in neighboring Pennsylvania and New Jersey, encouraging real estate developers to consider Delaware. None are doing so with more zeal than Amazon—the report cites Newmark Research showing Delaware ranks number two for the company—behind only San Antonio, Texas—in terms of square footage under development. You can see why Amazon finds it attractive as a distribution hub. It's surrounded by areas with lots of people and lots of wealth. The U.S. Census, in fact, considers Wilmington a part of the Philadelphia metro area, with many Delaware residents commuting to jobs there. Places like Rehoboth Beach, meanwhile, long a vacation spot for federal employees from Washington, DC, is now a popular retirement community for people in New Jersey, fleeing high property taxes. To be clear, Delaware certainly isn't a sunbelt-like growth story in terms of population, retiree migration and GDP expansion. Nor is Wilmington a millennial magnet like Boston, New York and Washington. But going forward, the presence of so many bankers and chemical engineers, plus the easy Amtrak access to other Northeast Corridor mega-cities, makes the state—and Wilmington more specifically—a place to watch for fintech and STEM-related startups.

(16)

LAS VEGAS, NEVADA

May 2021

The strange thing about the economic crisis of 2020? Most of America's leading industries had a great year. (Housing, finance, autos, manufacturing, technology, media…). This, however, won't make Las Vegas feel any better. Because its economy is all about leisure and tourism, and it's the leisure and tourism sector where much of last year's economic pain was concentrated. The city's airport welcomed just 22m people in 2020, versus 52m the year before. That meant lots of empty hotel rooms, casinos, restaurants and theatres. When the pandemic first hit last spring, the Las Vegas-area unemployment rate reached an incredible 33%. It's now down to more like 9%, but that's still a full three points above the national average. It's also, incidentally, a lot higher than in Reno, another Nevada city once overly dependent on tourism. Reno has since diversified, so much so that it's actually one of the nation's hotter economies right now. Reno-area household incomes have risen 45% in the past seven years, according to Mike Kazmierski of the Economic Development Authority of Western Nevada, speaking at a recent online event. Tesla has a big battery factory there. Amazon has a fulfillment center. And gaming revenue in Reno is now growing again—being within driving distance of the ultra-wealthy San Francisco Bay area certainty helps. Back in Vegas, leisure and hospitality jobs accounted for 29% of all non-farm employment on the eve of the pandemic, according to Labor Department data. In Phoenix, by contrast, the figure was just 11%. Las Vegas, remember, was harder hit than most economies by the 2008 housing meltdown—it had one of the country's biggest housing bubbles. This time, the Vegas housing market is strong despite the weak job market. Mercifully, visitors are starting to come again. Still, Bob Potts, deputy director for Nevada's economic development department, emphasizes the need for more Reno-like diversification. The fact is, gaming is becoming a more competitive sector, with competition from other locations and no less threateningly from the online world. Being so close to California and its giant economy is an immense advantage for Vegas as it looks to lure new industries, says Potts. The city also stands to benefit from Nevada's growth in clean energy production thanks to solar power. The state, which was dependent on mining before it was dependent on tourism, also happens to have lithium deposits now extremely valuable as battery material. Nevada is also a low tax state, especially relative to California. It's now home to many computer data centers. Nellis Air Force base is in the Vegas metro. So is the University of Las Vegas, Nevada (UNLV). And in Clark County, where Las Vegas is located, the biggest employer is actually the local school system, which saw rapid expansion as the Vegas metro area population grew a brisk 16% in the 2010s. It's now big enough to have an NFL football team (the Raiders). Interestingly, unlike in most metros, health care plays a relatively small role in the Vegas job market—Potts suggests health facilities simply haven't been able to expand fast enough to keep pace with population growth. But health care jobs are for sure a priority in the diversification efforts. As for the big casino resorts, companies like Sands, MGM and Wynn are indeed the area's largest private sector employers. Casino jobs tend to be union jobs too, if not quite replicating the impact unions had on the national labor market during the industrial era.

17

GARY, INDIANA

May 2021

Let's be frank: The story of Gary, Indiana isn't a happy one. The city didn't even exist in the 1800s. Only in the early 1900s did it appear on maps, after US Steel built a factory there. But in those days, that was like getting a new Amazon headquarters. It meant plentiful middle-class jobs and an influx of wealth. US Steel, after all, was for a time one of the world's largest and richest corporations, with links to some of America's most famous business magnates, most importantly Andrew Carnegie and JP Morgan. Just how important was steel to America's economy in the first half of the 20th century? It was essential to making cars, planes, railroads, skyscrapers and weapons. Just how important was it to the U.S. Midwest specifically? Pittsburgh has a football team named the Steelers. Gary itself is named for none other than Elbert Henry Gary, a founder of U.S. Steel. The point is, Gary was a Silicon Valley or Austin of its time, its steelmaking essential to running the American economy and winning both world wars. It's not long after the Second World War, however, that the story starts to sadden. Like the textile mills of New England before, the steel mills of the Midwest began losing out to lower-cost foreign competition. At the same time, racial tensions simmered amid an influx of Black Americans escaping the South for factory jobs in the North; many of these jobs were also filled by eastern European immigrants. As Gary's Black population grew, what followed was a textbook example of White flight to surrounding suburbs, incentivized by laws, regulations and practices affecting the real estate market. Nearby suburbs, furthermore, won state exemptions to incorporate, assuring Gary wouldn't have access to their tax base. People left. Companies left. Jobs left. Today, African Americans account for nearly 80% of Gary's 75k people. That 75k is 7% below what it was just ten years ago and about 100k below its peak in the 1960s. As for US Steel, it's sure enough still the city's largest employer. But where it once provided more than 30,000 jobs, it now has more like 7,000. The jobs, furthermore, don't provide the same compensation and social protections they once did. Today, just 2% of the population is foreign-born. Just half of residents own their homes. More than 30% fall below the poverty line. Less than two-thirds of homes have broadband internet. Perhaps nothing captures Gary's decline better than a comparison of downtown photos from the 1950s and today. The city, it seems, will never be the hub of prosperity it once was. But it *can* be better than it is today. Hope for a turnaround was on display last week, as Gary opened a new $300m Hard Rock casino. On hand for the ceremony: members of the original Jackson Five, brothers of Gary's most famous if controversial son, the late Michael Jackson. Smartphone manufacturer Akyumen Industries is moving its California-based headquarters to Gary, creating more than 2,000 jobs. Trucking and logistics companies, enjoying the ecommerce boom, are investing in the area given its proximity to Chicago (the downtown loop is just a 40-minute drive away). There's even good news on the steel front, with Alliance Steel moving its headquarters and processing plant to Gary. Officials in the meantime are prioritizing the removal of the city's many abandoned and blighted buildings and houses, hoping to attract new residents and businesses. Another priority is developing Gary's seven miles of Lake Michigan shoreline. The local airport, though it never caught on as an alternative gateway for Chicagoland, has at times attracted some scheduled service to places like Orlando. Much grander hopes lie with the Biden Administration's plans for infrastructure and family aid, many designed to address the problems of hard-hit places like Gary. It's a place that badly wants to get past being a metaphor for deindustrialization. As its local government slogan makes clear, it wants to reimagine the city.

18

WICHITA, KANSAS

May 2021

To understand the economy of Wichita, it helps to look down. Below the surface, in the city's outskirts, lies oil. But to really understand what makes the city tick today, look up. If you see an airplane, chances are, big parts of it were manufactured in Wichita. The area's largest employer, in fact, is Spirit AeroSystems, once part of Boeing and still the producer of its B737 fuselages. It's joined by other aerospace companies like Textron Aviation, which builds private planes. Canada's Bombardier has a major Wichita presence. So does GE Aerospace and Europe's Airbus. Manufacturing, as a result, accounts for nearly 16% of all Wichita jobs, according to Census data; that's barely less than the percentage tied to health care and education. McConnell Air Force Base further amplifies Wichita's aviation credentials. So does Wichita State University's National Institute for Aviation Research (NIAR), a big recipient of federal funding. Dr. Eric Mota, an entrepreneurship professor at Wichita State's Barton School of Business, highlights the city's outsized share of the Defense Department's budget, especially for aviation related maintenance, repair and overhaul. Mota, also a research fellow with the university's Institute for the Study of Economic Growth, adds that Wichita's aerospace prowess is now enabling a move into specialized manufacturing for other highly regulated industries, including energy and pharmaceuticals. His colleague Ted Bolema, the execute director of the Institute, names some other big employers in the city, including the energy-focused conglomerate Koch Industries, often in the news for its political activities. Cargill, a giant in the agricultural sector, has a big Wichita presence. As in so many other places across America, Amazon will soon open a new Wichita distribution center. Also like other U.S. areas, the local hospital and school districts are leading employers. Earlier this month, two Wichita-based banks—Equity Bank and American State Bank—announced a merger. Naturally, they'll count the area's aerospace firms among their biggest customers. But that, make no mistake, isn't a good thing right now. "The credit that we were most worried about," Equity Bank told investors last fall, "is aerospace." Even as pandemic-slammed sectors like tourism and leisure start to rebound, aerospace remains depressed, posing a major challenge to Wichita's economy. The sector was already reeling pre-pandemic after Boeing was forced to ground its best-selling B737 MAX planes in early 2019 after two fatal accidents. Wichita's unemployment today does remain below the national average at about 5%. But that masks major job losses in aerospace. Bolema points out that the market for business and private jets is starting to show signs of recovery. The oil and gas sector has improved a lot since the early days of Covid. But several longterm challenges remain. One is keeping and attracting skilled workers. The Wichita metro area saw its population grow less than 3% for the entire 2010s, finishing the decade with just 640,000 people. That ranks it 95th among all U.S. metros, sandwiched between Toledo, Ohio, and Augusta, Georgia. With so few people, the largest city in Kansas simply doesn't have the downtown living, the cultural amenities, the major league sports teams and so on to attract and retain large numbers of young engineers and other skilled workers. Many choose cities like Denver or Seattle instead. Another issue is the city's limited airline connectivity. Still another is its relative isolation—the nearest major population center is Oklahoma City, about 160 miles away. Kansas City is some 200 miles away, Dallas and Denver much farther still. Of course, affordable housing is a plus. And vigorous local efforts are underway to advance what Mota calls the "tripod" of economic development: investment, tourism and talent, perhaps aided by new trends in remote working. Wichita, to be sure, has come a long way from its origins as a cowboy cattle town in the 1870s. Oil gave it the means to seed what's become a world-class hub for aerospace. It's a status many cities envy. But dependence on aerospace means Wichita is subject to the industry's periodic busts, none more painful than the current one.

19

MIAMI, FLORIDA

May 2021

They come for the weather. They come for the beaches. Now, they're coming to start and run companies too. Count Miami as one of 2020's economic winners, luring an impressive list of high-powered financial and tech firms from New York and California. Blackstone, the esteemed private-equity group, moved its technology hub to Miami. Japan's SoftBank, a giant in venture technology investments, has a new Latin America fund based in Miami. Goldman Sachs is moving some jobs there. Microsoft will open a new office. And so on. But will the influx continue? City mayor Francis Suarez calls it more than just a moment but a movement. Perhaps some did come just because Florida was a good place to be outdoors during a pandemic. The state, furthermore, had fewer health-related operating restrictions on businesses and schools. By last fall, the state's economy was largely reopened. But the city—as well as the wider Dade County area—insist there are more enduring reasons for Miami's appeal, ones which remain relevant even as the pandemic passes. Florida's taxes, for one, are low (it's one of just nine states without a personal income tax). The airport is among the nation's 20 busiest, with unbeatable connections to Latin America and a broad menu of nonstop flights to Europe and even the Middle East. American Airlines, in fact, is Miami Dade's largest employer outside of the government, health and education sectors. If you're doing business in Latin America, you almost need to have a presence in Miami—this helps explain why some 1,300 multinational firms have offices there, according to Miami-Dade Beacon Council, a private-public partnership tasked with promoting economic development. According to the Council's executive VP of business development James Kohnstamm, the county is attracting as many as 1,000 new residents a week, while last year ranking seventh nationwide for venture capital investment. The area is home to multiple "unicorn" startups valued over $1b, including REEF technology and Cyxtera. Even putting aside the aviation jobs, plus the jobs tied to Latin American trade and the growing finance and tech sectors, Miami's economy is by any standards well-diversified. Tourism is of course vital, driving not just airline, hotel and restaurant employment but also a big cruise sector—Carnival, Royal Caribbean and Norwegian are all headquartered in Dade County. The area is home to several fast-food giants too, including Burger King and soon Subway. Ford chose Miami as its first testing site for autonomous vehicles. The container port is America's eleventh busiest. South Florida is certainly no stranger to the housing boom now evident nationwide. The area comprising the Miami housing market, as defined by the Department of Housing and Urban Development (HUD), is remarkably diverse in all senses of the word. Leisure and hospitality accounted for just 12% of jobs in 2019, compared to 16% for education and health. The number was 15% for professional and business services. It was 12% for government. A HUD report, meanwhile, notes that Miami is the only market in the U.S. where more than half of the total population is foreign-born. Also important at a time when many companies and entrepreneurs are eager to diversify their talent pool, Miami's Florida International University (FIU) ranks number one in the U.S. for Hispanic engineering graduates, with a high ranking for Black engineers as well. Officials and philanthropists are now directing more money to IT-related subjects at both FIU and the University of Miami. That said, the area arguably does punch below its weight in higher education, at least with respect to hosting the very upper tier of elite universities likely to attract the world's top students and future entrepreneurs. This is perhaps a legacy of Miami's original attraction as a place for retirees, a group for which education generally isn't a top priority. Another thing Miami lacks is a large manufacturing sector. It's considered among the most vulnerable U.S. cities to climate change. Many of its tourism jobs are low paid. With the protected Everglades to its west and the ocean to its east, Miami's physical expansion is constrained—other cities in Florida are growing faster. As an example, the Miami metro grew its population 10% in the 2010s; Orlando grew 22%. Then again, Miami is a much larger metro, the country's seventh largest in fact when including Broward and Palm Beach counties to the north. In a way, Miami's economy is both blessed and cursed by its geography. Yes, it helps to be a warm-weather place with lots of great beaches. But even aside from its worrying exposure to rising sea levels and intense heat, Miami's position in the far southeastern corner of the nation puts it far away from the U.S. west coast, far away from Europe and especially far from East Asia. A company doing business in Latin America? Sure, there's no better place than Miami. But for Asia, a much larger market, other cities are more attractive as bases. In any case, that doesn't seem to be a problem for all the finance and tech firms now coming and launching. Is it happening on an Austin- or Nashville-like scale? Not quite. But for Miami, the trend is in the right direction. The tourism sector, meanwhile, is already seeing a vigorous recovery. And the momentum will accelerate when cruises restart, perhaps this summer pending controversies over whether to allow vaccinated passengers only. As Kohnstamm makes clear, the cruise sector is a major economic force, encompassing a whole ecosystem of suppliers, dockworkers, service providers, entertainers and so on. A final step in Miami's post-Covid recovery will be a reopening of borders with countries in the Caribbean and South America.

FRESNO, CALIFORNIA

June 2021

You know about Silicon Valley. You know about Hollywood. But there's more to California than microchips and movies. Away from the coastline and beyond the mountains lies a valley, a valley with what just might be the most fertile agricultural land on planet earth. California is indeed an agricultural powerhouse, led by the prodigious output of its Central Valley. Fresno, with roughly a million people in its metro area, ranks 55th among all U.S. metros. Yet Fresno County produced more agricultural output than any other county in the nation—nearly $8b worth in 2019, according to the California Department of Food and Agriculture. Nearby counties in the San Joaquin section of the Central Valley produced almost as much, making the region as a whole America's undisputed leader in farming. The Fresno area itself is America's largest producer of almonds and raisins, to name just two products. Others produced in great quantity include pistachios, grapes, cotton, cattle, tomatoes, milk, plums, turkeys, oranges, peaches and nectarines. Much of the output (roughly a quarter) is exported abroad. The area, furthermore, is unsurprisingly home to many food-related businesses engaged in canning, curing, freezing and so on.

This, however, doesn't translate into high incomes. Fresno, on the contrary, is poorer per capita than not just the wealthy coastal cities of California but also the national average. Census data show median household income was $54,000 during the latter half of the 2010s, compared to San Francisco's $112,000 and $63,000 for the U.S. nationwide. Just 21% of Fresno's population has a college degree—the figure in San Francisco is 58%, the figure nationally is 32%. A fifth of people live in poverty, double the national rate. Interestingly, in 2006, the president of the San Francisco Federal Reserve brance came to Fresno and pointed out how most high poverty places in the U.S. were shrinking, i.e., Appalachia, the Mississippi Delta, Rust Belt cities like Detroit, etc. The Central Valley, by contrast, was growing rapidly at the time, and maintained a steady pace throughout the 2010s. That Fed official by the way, was current Treasury Secretary Janet Yellen. More than half of Fresno County's residents identify as Hispanic, and many are seasonal farm workers from Mexico. Mexican workers began coming as early as World War I. During World War II, the U.S. established the "Bracero" program allowing farms to hire guest workers during a time when many able-bodied Americans were off fighting. The Atlantic estimates that by 2014, 38% of Fresno's immigrants were undocumented. In general, while farm output has steadily grown in the 2000s, the number of farm workers has not. As the high level of undocumented workers suggests, labor shortages are a persistent attribute of farming in the Central Valley, and famers have auto-mated tasks to the extent possible. But they face something more alarming than labor shortages. They face severe water shortages. As the San Francisco Fed reported in last week's Fed Beige Book, "growers in California noted that current drought conditions are expected to negatively impact annual crops this year, driving up labor and electricity costs as farmers depend more on wells and water pumps for irrigation." That's poised to further increase food prices for all Americans. Fortunately, there's more than just farming in Fresno. As in most U.S. places, health and education jobs play an outsized role in the labor force, with Community Medical Centers the area's largest employer. Tourists traveling to Yosemite National Park often go via Fresno. Southwest Airlines, meanwhile, just launched flights to Fresno. Sure enough, the area has become a useful site for e-commerce fulfillment with

The Gap and Ulta Beauty recently opening warehouses. And of course, so did Amazon, in 2018. It helps that Los Angeles and San Francisco are both roughly just three hours by truck. Fresno stands to get another boost as an early stop on California's high-speed rail network. That will be a while. But the Bay Area Council Economic Institute, for one, sees the railway as an opportunity to position Fresno as a commuter town for Bay Area tech workers. It's also seen by boosters as a rare place in California that's not prohibitive to live and start a company. For now, though, agriculture remains front and center for Fresno. And for agriculture, water remains front and center. Pray for rain.

HAMPTON ROADS, VIRGINIA

June 2021

E nglish settlers started coming here more than 400 years ago. Today, nearly 2m people live in the Hampton Roads region of Virginia, making it the 38th largest metro in America. When it comes to U.S. national defense, however, and projecting U.S. military might abroad, few if any places nationwide have a greater importance than Hampton Roads. The number of active-duty military personnel stationed there is currently about 88,000. Naval Station Norfolk—the largest naval base in the world—alone has more than 47,000 active-duty personnel. Roughly 15% of the area's residents are military veterans—that's the twice the national average. Virginia Beach, specifically, is popular among military retirees. The broader metro including Norfolk and Newport News (and portions that dip into North Carolina) host no fewer than 15 military installations representing all five branches of the military. There's Fort Story. There's the Naval Air Station Oceana. There's Langley Air Force Base. And there's the area's massive shipbuilding facilities, including the Norfolk Naval Shipyard and the Newport News Shipyard. The latter is operated by a private-sector company called Huntington Ingalls, the largest U.S. shipbuilder and one of the country's largest recipients of federal contracts. It's also the world's only manufacturer of nuclear-powered aircraft carriers, not exactly a low-tech endeavor. There's also the high-tech nuclear physics lab, plus a major NASA research facility. Yet Hampton Roads hasn't evolved into a high-tech hub for private sector startups, like Silicon Valley famously did with help from funds flowing in from defense contracts. One reason is that the number of active military personnel is down by more than 20% from its peak in the early 2000s. In fact, during the 2010s, the metro area's population grew a mere 3%. Hampton Roads also lacks an elite university, though Old Dominion makes important contributions. It probably doesn't help economically that the Hampton Roads population is split across several cities, with Virginia's capital Richmond also not far. Only 7% of the population is foreign born, compared to 13% statewide and higher still in the D.C. suburbs. The bottom line: Military spending—and government more broadly—forms the nucleus of the economy. Government in fact accounts for a fifth of all jobs, similar to the ratio in Washington D.C.—Atlanta's figure, for example, is just 12%. The Port of Virginia, the third busiest on the east coast, is also government controlled (and currently booming). As for important private sector employers not associated with government contracting, Amazon sure enough announced several expansion projects in Hampton Roads last year. One will be a $200m robot-heavy fulfillment center slated to become the largest industrial building in Virginia. The retailer Dollar Tree is headquartered in Chesapeake. So are several food and beverage companies, including Smithfield Meats, one of the region's largest employers. But looking ahead, Hampton Roads is vulnerable to rising sea levels linked to climate change. According to the Rand Corporation, sea levels around Hampton Roads are one-to-two feet higher than they were a century ago, with floods now common in some coastal neighborhoods. Climate models, meanwhile, suggest the seas could rise by another 1.6 to 7.5 feet by the end of the century. In 2019, retired Rear Admiral Ann C. Phillips told Congress that "Virginia's high military concentration is tied to the water by the very nature of its mission, and at risk from the threat of sea level rise and climate change impacts." She also cited a 2008 OECD study that ranked the Hampton Roads metropolitan area as the 10th most vulnerable in the world based on the value of assets at risk from rising sea levels. (The top nine were Miami, Greater New York, New Orleans, Osaka-Kobe, Tokyo, Amsterdam, Rotterdam, Nagoya and Tampa-St Petersburg). On a more uplifting note, Hampton Roads stands to win plenty of new military contracts as the Navy, for its part, looks to modernize its vessels. The Port will expand in 2024. And offshore wind power is a growth sector. Ultimately though, the local economy's true power is power—America's military power.

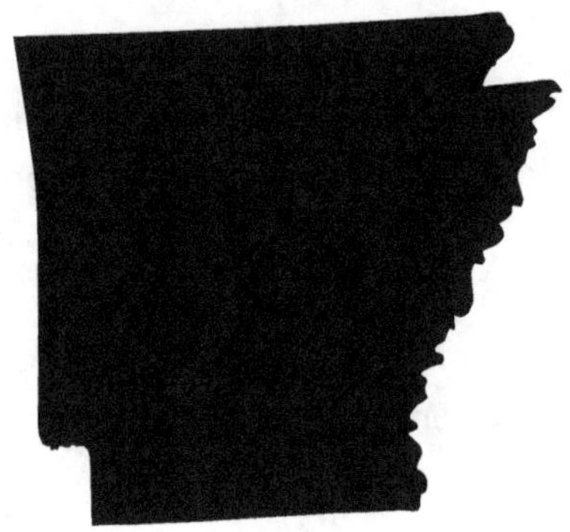

(2 2)

PINE BLUFF, ARKANSAS

June 2021

Of the nearly 400 metropolitan areas tracked by the U.S. Census, only one (outside of Puerto Rico) saw a double-digit decline during the 2010s. Pine Bluff, Arkansas, with 100,000 residents in 2010, had fewer than 88,000 by decade's end. That's a 12% drop. Even nearby Little Rock, hardly a fast-growing city, managed 6% growth in the 2010s. Why are so many people leaving Pine Bluff? In some ways, the city's decline mirrors those typically associated with the Midwestern rust belt—a story of industrial jobs that left for somewhere else or evaporated altogether. But Pine Bluff's problems are also representative of the wider Mississippi Delta region, and of rural areas overly dependent on farming and forestry. In its early years, Pine Bluff earned its living from slaves and cotton—cotton was the oil of its time, and the U.S. South its Saudi Arabia. Just as importantly, its location along the Arkansas River made the city an important shipping port, as it still is today. The river flows right into the Mighty Mississippi, which means crops and other commodities can easily and cheaply reach the critical port of New Orleans. Railroads would displace some river commerce but no worries—Pine Bluff became a major railroad hub and remains an important node in Union Pacific's network today. But jobs in manufacturing, agriculture and forestry disappeared over time, and the city began losing population as early as the 1980s. Pine Bluff also suffers from a serious crime problem, often labeled one of the dangerous places in the U.S. African Americans account for about half of the metro area's population, and about three quarters of the city itself. It was in fact the hometown of O.W. Gurley, who founded what came to be known as Black Wall Street in Tulsa. Efforts are now underway to recreate a version of that in downtown Pine Bluff, the site of numerous revitalization projects. Allison Thompson, CEO of the Economic Development Alliance for Jefferson County, highlights the downtown's new library, new art and performance space, a new aquatic center, additional housing and improved walkability. Just outside the city is a new casino that opened last fall and should create 1,000 new jobs. "We're pivoting to the jobs of today, not chasing the jobs of yesterday," said Thompson. Casinos, sure enough, are an increasingly popular way to generate jobs in areas of industrial decline (they're very labor intensive), especially in those where Amazon hasn't yet opened any fulfillment centers. Pine Bluff's port, meanwhile, is benefitting from a stronger post-Covid economy. And its job market is anchored by not just education and medical jobs but also federal and state government facilities. The National Center for Toxicological Research is the largest federal lab outside of Washington, DC. No less important is a major federal arsenal. The state's Department of Corrections, meanwhile, employs more than 1,400 people in the region. Tyson Foods is a major private-sector employer. So is Evergreen Packaging. And don't forget the many retail jobs supported by Walmart, the most famous Arkansas-based company (its home is Bentonville, a roughly four-hour drive from Pine Bluff). Agriculture remains important—Arkansas happens to be the number one rice producer in the U.S. A perennial threat, however, is flooding from the Arkansas River, including a costly one just two years ago.

DALLAS-FORT WORTH, TEXAS

June 2021

I n 1890, before the age of the automobile, Detroit was the 15th largest metro area in the U.S. By 1930, it ranked fourth, behind only New York, Chicago and Philadelphia. Two decades later, a Texas town best known for cowboys, railroads and cotton trading cracked the top 20 at number 15. Today, the twin cities of Dallas and Fort Worth have together matched Detroit's industrial-era achievement—the DFW Metroplex is now America's fourth largest metro area, behind only New York, Los Angeles and Chicago. Its Texas neighbor Austin sometimes gets more attention. Houston is booming too, supported by its giant energy sector. But DFW is larger than both, and it's *Exhibit A* of a superstar post-industrial sunbelt economy. Dallas got its start as the center of the early 20th century cotton trade. Already by 1914, it was economically important enough to house one of the 12 newly created Federal Reserve banks. Fort Worth, 30 miles to the west, was a hub for longhorn cattle trading since the 1860s, and meatpacking later on. A giant step to stardom came courtesy of the Texas oil boom in the 1920s. Though DFW didn't have any oil itself, its banks were instrumental in financing exploration and production elsewhere in the state. World War II proved economically transformative, as it was for so many cities across the U.S. Fort Worth in particular, became a major production site for military automobiles and aircraft. Well into the 1970s and 1980s, Fort Worth would be heavily dependent on the aerospace sector that emerged from those federal military investments—only after post-Cold War defense cuts did the city feel pressured to diversify into other areas. Dallas, meanwhile, received unwanted international attention as the site of President Kennedy's assassination in 1963. It would later enter the national consciousness for more prosaic reasons, including the Cowboys football team and the 1980s television show Dallas. In reality, the 1980s wasn't a great decade for DFW's economy. The drop in oil prices was felt throughout the state. And similarly damaging was the savings-and-loan banking crisis. But the one thing DFW always had: Its perfect location in the center of the country, just like Chicago to the north. But with population moving south and west, and with California emerging as the largest U.S. state, DFW was in some ways even more strategically located than the Windy City. It sure enough followed Chicago's lead in becoming one of the nation's most important transportation and logistics hubs. The railroads understood the geographic advantage in the 19th century, contributing to DFW's rise. And rail transport remains big business today—BNSF, the country's largest railroad (owned by Warren Buffet's Berkshire Hathaway), is headquartered in Fort Worth. No less importantly though, is DFW's nexus of interstate highways that make it critical to trucking and warehousing. Fort Worth, furthermore, is home to American Airlines, by some measures the world's largest airline. And Dallas is home to Southwest Airlines, famous for its low costs and nearly 50 straight years of profits before the pandemic (that's freakishly unheard of in the airline business). DFW airport was the world's tenth busiest in 2019, and the fourth busiest in pandemic-hit 2020. With so much rail, road and air transport, it's no wonder DFW—unlike most major cities throughout history—could thrive without any navigable links to the sea. Being so central also makes it a magnet for corporate headquarters, including many over the years that have relocated from New York and California. American Airlines and ExxonMobil, for example, were once New York City-based companies. Toyota North America and engineering giant Jacobs both moved from

California. So, more recently, did Charles Schwab and McKesson. AT&T moved from San Antonio. Seattle's Boeing nearly moved its head office to DFW before settling on Chicago. Aerospace nevertheless remains a big jobs provider, with Lockheed Martin alone employing more than 10,000 DFW residents. The military, health care and education sectors are large and stable employers. Finance remains critical too, with most major national banks having a big DFW presence. The area's "Silicon Prairie" is home to many tech companies, building on the legacy of Texas Instruments, an early IT superstar. With ExxonMobil, AT&T and McKesson, by the way, DFW is the only U.S. city to host three of the country's 15 largest companies. With so many job opportunities, and housing that's affordable relative to big coastal cities, DFW is understandably attracting people. Lots of them. During the 2010s, the Metroplex population grew 18%, second fastest among America's 20 largest metros (only Houston grew faster, slightly). In 2020, despite the pandemic, it saw the largest net increase of any area—120,000 more people from July 2019 to July 2020, according to newly released Census data. Since 2010, DFW has added 1.3m new people. And it wasn't because Texans are having a lot of babies. Last year, 48% of the increase came from domestic migration, and another 14% from international migration. Many of those from abroad come from Mexico and Central America, and Hispanics account for almost 30% of the DFW population today. A diverse population. A diverse economy. Both help make Dallas-Forth Worth the superstar economy it's become.

MADISON, WISCONSIN

July 2021

What do you call a Wisconsin city that's growing ten times the pace of its state's largest city? You call it Madison, whose metro area population grew 10% in the 2010s, far outpacing Milwaukee's 1%. If Milwaukee symbolizes a struggling midwestern rust belt economy, then Madison reflects the exact opposite: A fast-growing knowledge-based economy that looks more like Austin, the poster child for every ambitious city's aspirations. It's smaller, for sure. A lot smaller, with fewer than 700,000 people in the metro area. But like Austin, Madison has two stable bedrocks of economic might: 1) it's the seat of its state government and 2) it's home to a giant public university. In 2018, the state of Wisconsin employed more than 36,000 people in Madison, making it by far the area's largest employer. Number two, sure enough, is the University of Wisconsin (UW), with close to 15,000 employees, according to the U.S. Department of Housing and Urban Development (HUD). That doesn't even include the university's hospital (another 7,000-plus jobs). Government-sector jobs overall account for more than 21% of all Madison-area employment. And the university, including its hospital and its affiliated startup firms, claims its statewide economic impact amounts to some $15b. UW, meanwhile spent more than $1.1b on research and development in 2016, according to the National Science Foundation. With so much R&D and so many college-educated residents, it's no wonder that Madison, part of Dane County, has lots of tech startups relative to its smallish size. Median household income for Dane County? $74,000, compared to a national average of $63,000. The percentage of county residents with a college degree? 51%, compared to 32% nationally. Madison's success is sometimes overlooked amid the broader Wisconsin narrative—that it's a state known for family-owned farms producing dairy products like cheese. There's Milwaukee, of course, which only ranks number 40 among America's largest metros. As recently as 2005, noted the HUD in a recent report, manufacturing was still the largest employment sector in Milwaukee. But long gone are the days when German immigrants brewing beer and toiling in factories was a hallmark of economic dynamism. Livestock was always big business in Wisconsin. And packing the meat too—there's a reason they're called the Green Bay *Packers*. But none of this is representative of Madison. There, the median age is just 31. A tenth of residents commute using public transit. Inbound tourism makes a meaningful economic contribution. And during the pandemic, as tech talent fled big cities like San Francisco and New York, Madison proved an attractive lure. A LinkedIn study, furthermore, ranked it number one for cities that retained its tech talent during the Covid crisis. Its largest private employer, in fact, is a health care software company called Epic Systems. Being small has its advantages, including a lower cost of living. But it has its disadvantages too. Madison is a two-plus hour drive from Milwaukee, the nearest big city and airport. The nearest *hub* airport is almost three hours away in Chicago. Minneapolis is more than four hours by car. It's one reason why large companies won't put their headquarters in Madison. But no worries. Not when you have a giant university, and not when your city is the state capital.

SANTA FE, NEW MEXICO

July 2021

Within its own neighborhood, New Mexico's economy is distinctively undynamic. GDP grew an inflation-adjusted 13% during the 2010s, as the state's population increased less than 2%. During the same period, all four states surrounding New Mexico—Arizona, Texas, Colorado and Utah—saw their real GDPs increase at least 26% and their populations rise between 14% and 16%. Albuquerque is New Mexico's largest city. The state's Southwest includes the oil-rich Permian Basin most often associated with West Texas. Much of northwest New Mexico is home to Native American lands. The state is known for its federal research labs, including Los Alamos, originally established during World War II to develop an atomic bomb. And then there's one of the most unique places in the entire United States, with an economy no less distinctive. Santa Fe, the second oldest city in the U.S. after St. Augustine, Florida, was founded more than 400 years ago. Today it's home to just 85,000 people, or 150,000 including its surrounding area. But lots of tourists come to visit, making leisure and hospitality a staple of the local economy. The sector accounted for 18% of all jobs in 2018. And tourists underpin a vibrant retail trade that generates a sizeable portion of the city's tax revenue. But Santa Fe is also New Mexico's capital, which means government is a major economic force, responsible for perhaps a quarter of all jobs. The state of is by far the area's largest employer. Health care is a big sector, in part because Santa Fe is a popular retirement community—a quarter of all metro area residents are over the age of 65 (the figure statewide and nationwide is 18% and 17%, respectively). Unlike hotspot retirement communities in Arizona and Florida, however, Santa Fe's population growth during the 2010s was just 4%. That was double the lowly state average but still indicative of one important deterrent for prospective retirees: It's a rather expensive city, with home values above the national average. Many of Santa Fe's retirees, in fact, have highish incomes and come from wealthy states like California and Colorado. And sure enough, real estate is big business in Santa Fe. There's some nearby gold mining. The town is known for its vibrant art scene, one aspect of its tourist appeal. The tourists tend to come during the summer and fall, which makes for a highly seasonal economy. But they are coming again now that Covid is less of a threat, driving up tax revenues this year. Like most communities, Santa Fe is doing what it can to lure startups and technology companies. It's a site for some television and movie production too. Due to its topography, Santa Fe long ago lost its role as a major trading center connecting Mexico with Missouri. The Santa Fe railroad, despite its name, bypassed the city because of the engineering challenges associated with its mountainous terrain. Santa Fe, meanwhile, saw the closure of a federal military base in the 19th century. In the 21st century, the challenges are quite different and unique—one being the difficulty laying broadband cables in areas of archaeological significance.

GREENVILLE-SPARTANBURG, SOUTH CAROLINA

July 2021

Once upon a time, when Detroit was the world's center of auto manufacturing, Upcountry South Carolina was the world's center of textile manufacturing. After the Civil War, the railroads came to the foothills of the Blue Ridge Mountains, and so did New England and mid-Atlantic mill owners seeking lower labor costs. The aftermath of another war—World War II—would mark a slow and painful decline for the textile industry in Greenville and Spartanburg, not unlike the auto decline experienced in places like Detroit. Where did the textile industry go? Mostly overseas, to low-wage economies in East Asia and the Indian subcontinent. And where did the auto industry go? Many companies went to the American South, no less determined to find lower labor costs than their textile industry predecessors. To be precise, it wasn't America's auto giants that came—many were prevented from doing so by union contracts. Instead, their foreign competitors came. Mercedes Benz, Honda and Hyundai came to Alabama. Toyota came to Kentucky. Nissan and Volkswagen came to Tennessee. And

BMW came to Greer, South Carolina, situated just between Greenville and Spartanburg. The German carmaker arrived in 1992, putting the area on a road to becoming a manufacturing powerhouse. In 2018, BMW was employing 8,000 workers at its South Carolina factory, producing vehicles for both the domestic and export markets. In fact, BMW is today the largest car exporter from the U.S., with most of its products shipped via the port of Charleston to markets like China, South Korea, Russia and of course the company's home country Germany. Just as importantly for the local Greensboro-Spartanburg economy, the BMW plant drew many auto suppliers to the area, from Michelin (tires) to ZF (transmissions) to Bosch (powertrains). In 2014, according to a Housing and Urban Development report, BMW had a direct impact of $12.5b on South Carolina's economy. It's not *just* the non-union workforce and business-friendly conditions that BMW finds attractive. It's also Greenville-Spartanburg's location between Charlotte (less than two hours away by road) and Atlanta (roughly three hours). It's also close to the booming tourist and retirement community of Asheville in the Blue Ridge Mountains. Proximity to Charleston's world-class port facilities, too, are important. So is access to Charlotte and Atlanta airports, both with nonstop flights to BMW's home city Munich. The tens of thousands of lost textile jobs won't be forgotten. But the auto jobs make the memories less painful. Non-auto manufacturers are now coming as well, supplemented by large numbers of health care jobs. The restaurant chain Denny's is headquartered in the area. Just last month, Oshkosh Defense announced plans to build a $155m operation in Spartanburg, creating 1,000 new jobs to build electric delivery vehicles for the U.S. Post Office. China's Gissing announced an investment last month as well. Less happily for the region and its thriving manufacturing base, the U.S.-led tariff war had a dampening effect on further investment, especially from Germany and Japan. David Britt, chairman of the local economic development committee, told a recent discussion panel that BMW for one hasn't made any meaningful investments since the start of tariff hostilities. Nevertheless, Greenville-Spartanburg's economy is booming again. Britt speaks of $1.2b in new investment in just the past six months, creating 3,100 new jobs. People are coming for the jobs, plus the favorable weather and relatively low living costs. Just before the pandemic in 2019, the Greenville-Spartanburg airport saw record passenger traffic. As it happens, the two neighboring cities, if treated as one metro area, would be the state's largest with 1.2m people—that's after robust population growth of about 12% during the 2010s. Neither the capital Columbia nor Charleston itself has more people. Just how humming is the economy now as the Covid crisis recedes? In an interview with NPR's Marketplace, Britt made his assessment clear: "Things are far better than we ever imagined."

LEXINGTON, KENTUCKY

July 2021

Louisville is Kentucky's biggest city. Frankfort is the state's capital. Covington is home to its busiest passenger airport, which actually serves the Ohioan city of Cincinnati. Louisville's airport is the busiest in the world for shipping giant UPS. Lexington, however, has a few of its own economic advantages. Most importantly, it's home to the University of Kentucky, a school with more than 30,000 students and some 17,000 employees. It's a public university, though the majority of its revenue comes not from state tax dollars or even tuition, but rather from health care services operated by its affiliated hospital. Lexington also has what Greenville-Spartanburg has: A giant foreign auto plant, in its case owned by Japan's Toyota. The plant, in nearby Georgetown, employs roughly 10,000 people—it's Toyota's largest production facility anywhere in the world. But Lexington isn't best known for its colleges or factories. It's best known as the horse capital of the world, situated in the state's Bluegrass region just west of the Appalachian Mountain range. The Kentucky Derby, a famous horse race, is held in Louisville. But Lexington has its own popular racetracks, not to mention large horse auction markets. Bluegrass country is famous for its Bourbon distilleries too, which also attract tourists and retirees. In fact, Lexington's 9% population growth during the 2010s was almost double that of Louisville's rate. Amazon is a big employer in the region, as are Conduent (once part of Xerox) and Lexmark (once part of IBM). Lockheed Martin employs more than a 1,000 people in the area as well. Put it all together, and it's a rather well-diversified economy. According to the Department of Housing and Urban Development, government accounts for 20% of all jobs, professional services another 14% and health and education just 13%. Manufacturing (11%), retailing (11%) and leisure and hospitality (10%) are all important but not systemically so. Demographically, Lexington's metro area has similar percentages of White and Black residents as the national average. But its Hispanic and immigrant populations are significantly smaller. Education levels are quite high thanks to the university. Looking more broadly at Kentucky, the state faces economic challenges from its exposure to coal mining and tobacco. On the other hand, it's well situated for east coast distribution and logistics, which UPS and Amazon have figured out. The spectacular growth in ecommerce, therefore, is a boost for Kentucky. And for Lexington too.

BEND, OREGON

August 2021

I t's small by city standards. But perhaps not for long given current growth rates. Bend, an Oregon city southeast of Portland, saw its population grow an astounding 25% during the 2010s. And the 2020s are off to just as vivacious a start, with Bend appearing regularly on rankings of top places for resettlement and remote working during the pandemic. In fact, among the nearly 400 metro areas tracked by the U.S. Census, Bend's 25% growth last decade was topped by only six other places (The Villages, Austin, Myrtle Beach, Midland, St. George and Greeley—in Florida, Texas, South Carolina, Texas, Utah and Colorado, respectively). Why are so many people coming to Bend? For some the lure is affordability—many newcomers are people priced out of nearby Portland or other expensive cities like San Francisco and Seattle. Some are high-income tech workers buying second homes from which to work remotely. Some compare Bend to Aspen or Lake Tahoe, two better-known resort towns popular with prosperous westerners. Tourism, sure enough, accounts for about 17% of Bend's economy, according to EDCO, an economic development group for Central Oregon. Its chief Roger Lee, like all econ development leaders these days, speaks of Austin as the holy grail of development success. But in Bend's case, Boulder is more apt for comparison given its size. Even Boulder though, has an easier time attracting businesses thanks to how close it is to Denver (just 30 minutes by car); Bend is about three hours from Portland. Still, the area is attracting smaller industries and companies, including some in the cannabis sector. Natural foods is another important sector for Bend, which is home for example to Laired Superfood. The city has small tech startups too, including several focused on video games. The biggest employers, however, are the city's resorts, led by Sunriver. Bend's largest employer of all is St. Charles Health System—here again an example of just how vital health care is to the American labor market. Ditto for education and government; Central Oregon Community College, a public school, is Bend's third largest employer after St. Charles and Sunriver. Another big employer—the manufacturer Bright Wood—lies just north of Bend in Madras. Unsurprisingly, Bend's affordability is now challenged by soaring home prices. Lee points to nearby Prineville, just 35 miles away, where home prices are much cheaper. Oregon in general has a stark urban-rural divide, and a history of tense political fights over environmental measures that have in some cases hurt the state's important timber and logging industry. A final demographic note about Bend: Its population is 93% White, compared to 87% for Oregon as a whole and 76% for the entire U.S.

LOS ANGELES, CALIFORNIA

August 2021

I n 2019, Los Angeles County alone had an economy worth \$727b. That's larger than the GDPs of Saudi Arabia or Switzerland. And it makes the broader L.A. metro area America's second largest economy—only New York City's is larger. How did a town that barely existed in the 19th century rise to such extraordinary heights in the 20th and 21st? It wasn't the California gold rush—that (during the 1840s) triggered the rise of San Francisco. L.A. experienced a different sort of gold rush in the 1890s, specifically "black gold," or oil. Before the age of Texas oil a few decades later, California was the country's largest producer, with L.A. and its surroundings playing a central role. As it happened, the oil discoveries came not long after L.A. was connected to the rest of the country by the transcontinental railroad. Before that, it was mostly a frontier town with some agricultural activity. Even earlier it was part of the Spanish empire and later Mexico, but always home to just a few thousand people at most. Oil, however, was a big catalyst to population growth. Competing railroads, meanwhile, slashed their fares to win westbound customers. Development of seaport facilities followed. Then came the highways and Hollywood. During the Great Migration of slave descendants out of the South, many African Americans from Louisiana migrated to Los Angeles (as personified by Dr. Robert Foster in Isabel Wilkerson's book "The Warmth of Other Suns"). Many came for the great weather. As a New Deal-era history described, "to many a newcomer, Los Angeles is a modern Promised Land." Already by then, the Culver City neighborhood was known for its motion picture studios. Long Beach had its oil wells. Pasadena and Beverly Hills were already retreats for the rich. Inglewood was already home to airplane factories. The San Pedro Bay was already a bustling seaport. The San Fernando Valley at the time featured many prosperous farms. By 1940, L.A. had become the fifth largest U.S. city after New York, Chicago, Philadelphia and Detroit. But L.A. hadn't seen anything yet. World War II, followed by the Cold War, would turn southern California into a giant center of defense-related manufacturing and research. Between the 1950s and the 1980s, California received roughly a fifth of all federal defense contracts, including money that seeded the rise of Silicon Valley to the north. In southern California, much of the money went to aviation and aerospace, creating a wealth of high-paying jobs. It didn't hurt that two southern Californians occupied the White House during much of the 1970s and 1980s, Richard Nixon and Ronald Reagan, respectively. But dependence on defense contracts proved troublesome during the Cold War cutbacks of the early 1990s, when L.A.'s economy suffered its first severe recession. During this period, the region also lost tens of thousands of clothing factory jobs. Foreign investment, furthermore, tumbled as Japan's economy turned from boom to bust. Before long though, L.A.'s abundance of engineering, science, professional and creative talent positioned it perfectly for the new information age. Just as importantly, the rise of China and Asia-based manufacturing cemented Los Angeles and Long Beach as America's largest and most important seaports. In 2019, L.A's main airport surpassed Chicago O'Hare to become the nation's second busiest after Atlanta. And that's despite its coastal geography which makes it impractical as a connecting hub. Air, sea, rail and road transportation are indeed a vital cog in L.A's economy today. So is tourism, including international tourism which remains depressed amid the pandemic. That—and international trade exposure more generally—is a big reason that L.A.'s metro area unemployment rate remains high at 9.5%, compared to 5.4% nationally (the July figure) and just 3.2% in Salt Lake City, for example. On the other hand, southern California's real estate market is red hot. Maybe *too* hot. In L.A.'s wealthy Westside housing market (which includes Beverly Hills, Hollywood, Malibu, Marina del Rey, Santa Monica, Venice, West Hollywood and Westwood), the *average* home sale price in mid-2020 reached $1.8m. Even in less exclusive neighborhoods, affordability is a giant problem, blocking opportunities for Americans to take advantage of L.A.'s many good jobs. The pattern of moving to California for a better life—a staple of national lore—seems to have died. The dominant historical pattern is now reversed: People *leaving* L.A. for cheaper housing markets, especially given the dispersion of job opportunities thanks to remote working. Some *companies* are leaving too, lured by lower taxes in states like Austin, Texas (which is now experiencing a housing affordability problem of its own). Another perennial challenge is nature, including L.A.'s vulnerable water supply and exposure to wildfires and earthquakes. Still another is the future of U.S.-China trade relations. On the other hand, L.A.'s Hollywood stars like Disney are still going strong (albeit uncertain about the longterm economics of video streaming). Defense contractors like Northrup Grumman remain big employers. Two giant universities—UCLA and USC—provide jobs to tens of thousands of residents. So do the area's many health care institutions, led by Kaiser Permanente. The City of Los Angeles is actually the metro area's second largest employer after UCLA, according to HUD. Silicon Valley's finest—Google, Apple, Facebook and so on—all have a major presence in the City of Angels. Oddly enough, one institution that *doesn't* have a prominent L.A. presence is the Federal Reserve. This reflects how economically unimportant the city was when the Fed was created a century ago. Year after year in ensuing decades, L.A. kept on growing and growing and growing, with people coming from all over America and the world. The city now has neighborhoods with nicknames like Koreatown, Little Armenia and Little Tokyo. Some jokingly call it Tehrangeles for its many Iranian Americans. East L.A. is arguably the capital of Mexican-American culture. Whereas east coast cities saw early development with waves of immigrants from Europe, L.A.'s growth was fueled more by immigration from Mexico,

Central America, Asia and the Middle East. But again that question: Can people still afford to come? Affordable housing, to be sure, will rank high among the forces shaping L.A.'s future economic growth. It has so many of the other elements of success already in place: its attractive weather, its giant transport facilities, its tourist appeal, its established immigrant communities, its pool of highly educated workers, etc. No need to be jealous of Austin *here*. But with the days of mass building houses and freeways long gone, L.A. and California more broadly will need new solutions, perhaps aided by new government policies and new construction technologies. What will L.A. look like seven years from now? The city will reclaim the global spotlight when it hosts the 2028 Olympics, just as it did in 1984, at the height of its golden years. Is there another Golden State golden era coming?

(3 0)

INDIANAPOLIS, INDIANA

August 2021

oosier basketball. Peyton Manning and the golden era of Colts football. The world's most famous speedway. For a city not even large enough for a Major League Baseball team, Indianapolis is nevertheless a sports colossus. You could see it earlier this year when the city hosted the entire March Madness college basketball tournament. The Indianapolis Motor Speedway, seating some 260,000 people, is the largest sporting venue in the world. Sports, according to a 2014 estimate by Indiana and Purdue Universities, generate $3.4b in annual direct spending for the Indianapolis metro area, not to mention support for nearly 10,000 jobs. Sports are not, however, the defining characteristic of America's 33rd largest metro area. There's a lot more to its economy, which stands out—along with its Ohio neighbor to the east Columbus—as one of the Midwestern region's all-stars. The Midwest is often defined not by its all-stars but by its troubled giants, most prominently Detroit. But Indianapolis never relied on manufacturing jobs to quite the same extent. Unlike Detroit, for starters, it's a state capital. That alone provides an economic base of 35,000 state government employees. It's a big base of *federal* government operations too, specifically the

General Services Administration. But government employment is hardly the only prerequisite to a city's success—look at depressed state capitals like Trenton in New Jersey. Indianapolis is much more than a government town. Its largest private sector employer is the pharmaceutical giant Eli Lilly. It's also a leading transportation hub thanks to its location—less than 200 miles from Chicago, Columbus, Louisville, Dayton and Cincinnati. Add another 100 miles and you're in the radius of Detroit, St. Louis, Milwaukee and Nashville. Few cities have as much importance to the trucking industry, perhaps not surprising given all the interstate highways that meet there. It's a major intermodal rail hub for CSX. Indianapolis airport, though not a major passenger hub, happens to host Fedex's largest operation after Memphis. Naturally, as a transportation hub, warehouse activity is bustling—Indianapolis is an important distribution center for Amazon, Walmart and the supermarket giant Kroger. Indiana, to be clear, suffered deeply from America's shift from a manufacturing to service-based economy. According to the Indianapolis Star, citing data from the Bureau of Economic Analysis, the state lost 235,000 manufacturing jobs between 1969 and 2014. That was almost a third of all its manufacturing jobs. But much of that happened outside of Indianapolis, in cities like Gary. Within the Indianapolis metro, auto suppliers remain vibrant, led by companies like Allison Transmission. Foreign manufacturers like Rolls-Royce have a major presence in the area. Notably large is the foreign software services company Infosys from India. Simon Property is another big Indy-based company. Salesforce, though based in San Francisco, has a large Indy office. But that's not all. The city has become a major regional financial center, with outsized importance in the insurance sector. Anthem, most importantly, is one of the nation's largest medical insurers. Indianapolis more generally has a large professional and business service sector, which usually means high average incomes. And never forget about the health and education sectors, always accounting for a large portion of a city's total jobs. For companies considering a move, Indiana is notably aggressive in luring companies with business-friendly policies, often contrasting itself with neighboring Illinois. What it can't do is lure many retirees looking for sunshine—those folks are going to the sunbelt. As a result, population growth isn't quite Florida like. But with lots of good jobs, the population of metro area Indianapolis grew a healthy 10% in the 2010s. The good jobs attract educated millennials and Gen Z folks too, with efforts underway to become even more attractive by improving transport and entertainment facilities downtown. The pandemic of course hurt. But the subsequent federal stimulus helps, especially so with all the money allocated for state governments. As Indiana's state capital, Indianapolis stands to benefit. Now if only the Colts can get back to the Super Bowl.

(31)

ATLANTIC CITY, NEW JERSEY

August 2021

There are cities whose best days lie ahead. There are cities whose best days are long past. Atlantic City, sadly, is fighting an uphill struggle to elude the latter category. Today, all one needs is a single word to capture the essence of its economy: Casinos. But unlike Las Vegas, where casino growth coincided with a population and economic boom, Atlantic City remains a city mired in deep poverty, with a metro-area population that shrank 4% during the 2010s. The city itself had a poverty rate of 37% in 2019, compared to just 9% for all of New Jersey, one of America's wealthiest states. Median annual income was just $29,000, compared to $83,000 statewide (and $63,000 nationwide). There's some resemblance to other northeast cities, from Philadelphia to Baltimore to New Jersey's own Newark and Trenton, all of which likewise experienced a major post-World War II outflow of people, especially middle-class Whites (Atlantic City's population peaked in the 1930 Census). But today, these other cities all have many highly prosperous suburbs nearby. Atlantic City does not. Most of New Jersey's wealth resides farther north. What Atlantic City does have are beaches, an allure recognized as early as the 1850s. It seemed an ideal location, developers at the time concluded, for the monied classes of New York and Philadelphia to spend the summer. The advent of rail transportation made this possible. And sure enough, Atlantic City became one of the nation's first major tourist destinations. Its famous boardwalk opened in 1870. During the prohibition era of the 1920s, it became a magnet for organized crime. The Great Depression came next, battering economies everywhere. Then came world war in the 1940s. But Atlantic City never experienced the post-war economic boom enjoyed elsewhere. By the 1950s, most affluent Americans had their own cars to drive, giving them more vacation choices. As air travel developed—and especially cheap air travel after airline deregulation in the 1980s—Florida and the Caribbean became the go-to spot for beaches. Airlines also gave gambling-minded northeasterners easy and affordable access to Las Vegas. To give Atlantic City a fighting chance, New Jersey—in 1976—legalized casino gambling. Two years later, Resorts International opened the city's first casino hotel. To a degree, the plan worked. The 1980s saw a frenzy of new investment, most famously by a New York real estate developer named Donald Trump (you may have heard of him). Atlantic City would gain renewed national notoriety for its Miss America pageants and championship boxing matches—in 1988, Mike Tyson became the undisputed heavyweight champion of the world at the Atlantic City convention center, beating Michael Spinks. But Spinks wasn't the only one to get painfully punch: The recession of the early 1990s hit Atlantic City hard. It would bankrupt Trump's casino empire and discourage new investment. Still, the number of visitors grew in the 1990s, if only a modest 4%, reaching 33m by 2000, according to data from the University of Nevada Las Vegas (nearly all visitors come by car or tour bus). But then came another punch: A wave of new casino competition throughout the northeast, some operated by Native American tribes. In the Philadelphia metro area alone, three new casinos opened between 2007 and 2010. As a result of the new competition, from 2006 through 2016, the number of casinos in Atlantic City declined from 12 to just seven. In 2017, annual visits totaled just 24m, the lowest figure since 1982, according to Stockton University. The peak for arrivals was 2005, when about 35m came. In 2014, meanwhile, gross gambling revenue was down 53% percent compared with the all-time peak of $5.2b in 2006.

The decline, which convinced Apple for one to close its store on the city's boardwalk, didn't however dissuade two new casinos from opening in 2018, creating about 8,000 new jobs. Bad timing though: The 2020 pandemic hit Atlantic City's economy harder than almost anywhere in the U.S. The area ranked number three nationwide for employment loss, leaving a third of the metro area's labor force jobless (the figure was more like 50% for the city itself). As casinos reopened this year, jobs have returned, but metro area unemployment remains elevated at 11%. Leisure and hospitality, by the way, account for 30% of the region's unemployment, with others mostly employed in government, education, health or transportation. Atlantic City does have a Federal Aviation Administration facility that employs nearly 4,000 people, making it the region's largest non-casino employer. (Caesars is the largest among the casinos). AtlantiCare, Shore Medical Center and Stockton University are other notable jobs providers. In addition, some 10,000 people own second homes in Atlantic City, boosting the economy during the summer tourist season. Spirit Airlines offers Atlantic City flights to Florida, Atlanta and Myrtle Beach. Is it too pessimistic to say that Atlantic City's best days are behind it? The two new casinos offer hope. So does New Jersey's recent legalization of online gambling and sports betting, giving Atlantic City's casinos new sources of revenue (though it's unclear if that new revenue will stay in the area). Had there been no casino legalization in the 1970s, Atlantic City would surely have attracted less investment. Yet for locals, the high poverty rate—along with other data like average home values and broadband access—reveals a story that looks much, much different from Las Vegas. Atlantic City remains—behind Vegas—the second largest commercial casino market nationwide. But the two are worlds apart in terms of population growth, economic diversification and global prestige. It does have great saltwater taffy though.

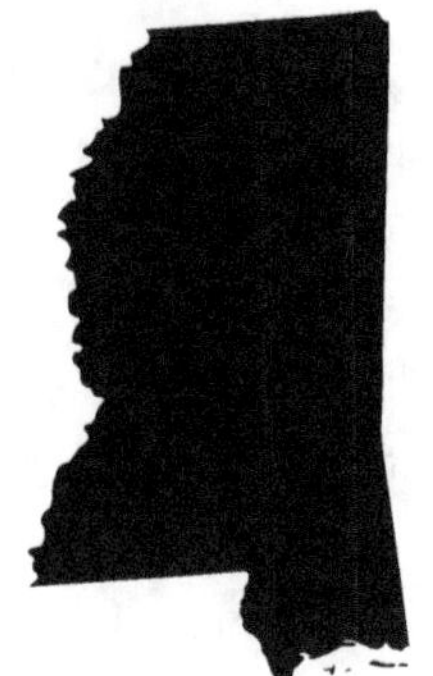

GOLDEN TRIANGLE, MISSISSIPPI

September 2021

Making steel. Building helicopters. Manufacturing engines. These are not things typically associated with Mississippi, by many measures the poorest U.S. state. But they're all indeed a feature of the economic landscape in a region dubbed the "Golden Triangle." It's not in the storied Mississippi Delta, one of the highest-poverty regions in America. Nor is it on the state's ecologically fragile Gulf Coast. The Golden Triangle lies in the east, close to the Alabama border. The Triangle itself includes Starkville, home to Mississippi State University and its more than 4,000 employees. There's West Point at the top of the triangle. There's Columbus, home to a U.S. Air Force base. And within the triangle: A surprising number of manufacturing facilities serving national and even global markets. It wasn't always this way. As late as 2007, the region was in the throes of a de-industrialization wave symbolized by the closure of an old meat processing plant that employed roughly a thousand people. But Joe Max Higgins was already hard at work. He's today one of the country's most celebrated economic development leaders, featured in media programs like "60 Minutes" and even a Harvard Business School case study. An early triumph was securing the Tennessee

Valley Authority's "megasite" certification for major industrial development. That ensured a steady supply of cheap electricity and a streamlined path for manufacturers looking to establish a presence. Put another way, it removed important elements of risk for companies A Russian steel manufacturer responded, opening a plant since sold to Indiana-based Steel Dynamics. Airbus, the European aerospace giant, owns a helicopter factory close to the steel plant. Not far away is a tire plant opened in 2015 run by Japan's Yokahama Tires. One selling point for the Golden Triangle is its proximity to the many auto manufacturing plants throughout the South. Sure enough, car companies are some of the largest buyers of Mississippi-built steel and tires. Paccar, which makes engines, is another area manufacturer catering to the auto sector. In total, Higgins and his team claim to have netted some 6,000 manufacturing jobs since the early 2000s, along with $5.5b in capital investment. No wonder why others see the area as a model for development. The biggest challenge is finding enough skilled workers to staff all the new manufacturing jobs. For all its success and job creation, the area hasn't seen much population growth and struggles to attract millennials, GenZers and immigrants. Mississippi State certainly helps, as does East Mississippi Community College, which works closely with manufacturers to help train people in specific skills as needed. Mississippi, incidentally, has the highest percentage of African Americans of any state, a legacy of the pre-Civil War era when much of its land was used for slave-based cotton farming. Nearly half of all residents in Lowndes County, home to many of the factories, are African American, making the area's success with job creation a potential template for improving racial equity. The Airbus factory, furthermore, employs many U.S. military veterans. Speaking earlier this year on the "Supertalk Mississippi" program, Higgins outlined his goal to attract more companies catering to outdoor sports like hunting and boating, both popular in the Golden Triangle. Another avenue of growth: Solar power farms; several are now in development. Even with all the corporate newcomers, the Golden Triangle offers just one nonstop airline route. But it happens to be to Atlanta, the busiest airport in the world. And that means easy one-stop access to most major business centers worldwide, including auto centers like Detroit, Frankfurt and Tokyo. The area is well connected, meanwhile, by highways, railways and even a canal to the Gulf coast port of Mobile that opened in 1985. An ample supply of land, lowish housing costs, mild winters and a nonunion labor force are other attractions for employers. Importantly, the state recently allocated heavy spending for upgrading broadband access. The Golden Triangle never did win a giant foreign auto manufacturing plant like, say, Greenville-Spartanburg with its BWM facility. (Nissan does have one near Mississippi's capital Jackson, and Toyota has one south of Memphis near Tupelo). But the Triangle has certainly benefited from the south's expanding auto industry exposure, and from modern manufacturing more generally.

BOISE, IDAHO

September 2021

For a front-row seat to some of America's most important economic and demographic trends, visit Idaho. Start with the housing crisis. No, not the one that broke the economy in the late 2000s. It's the one occurring right now in so many metro areas—an affordability crisis caused by demand far outpacing supply. In Boise, Idaho's capital, "homeownership is becoming increasing unaffordable." That's a direct quote from the Federal Department of Housing and Urban Development (HUD), which adds that home prices have been increasing faster than wages for the past nine years. Housing economists measure supply-and-demand conditions by estimating the number of months it would take for the current inventory of homes on sale to sell, given the current sales pace. Six months is considered a market in healthy balance. In Boise at the end of 2020, the brokerage Redfin notes, the figure was 0.3 months. The average sale price, meanwhile, jumped 15% y/y in the 12 months to November 2020, reaching $371,300, according to HUD. That's 27% greater than the pre-recession peak in 2007 and more than twice as much as the trough in 2009. This year, the surge has gone into overdrive—Barron's last week said median home prices rose an astonishing

41% y/y in Q2. People must really love potatoes. Well, not exactly. It *is* true that potato farming remains big in Idaho—the specialist J.R. Simplot is the Boise area's ninth largest employer. But there's a different reason why the area's population grew 21% during the 2010s, more than all but five other Top 100 metros nationwide (only Austin, Fort Myers, Raleigh-Durham, Provo and Orlando grew faster). The key reason is domestic migration of retirees from places with high costs of living. Boise welcomed the largest number of its net new arrivals from Los Angeles, followed by those fleeing San Diego, Denver, the Inland Empire and the San Francisco Bay Area. (Many retirees arrive from Portland and Seattle as well, though these are also places where many younger Boise natives look for jobs, hence a more balanced inflow and outflow). At present, residents aged 65 or older account for more than 15% of Boise's population, up from 10% in 2010. And therein lies another big national trend: The aging of America, which can influence everything from inflation to interest rates to government spending priorities. Of course, a big increase in retirees means a big increase in demand for health care, which has indeed created many new jobs in Boise and across the country. The area's largest employer, sure enough, is St. Luke's Health System. Also arriving, to be sure, are second-home buyers, often working remotely from Boise but earning high incomes in places like California. The newsletter "Full Stack" refers to cities like Boise as the Mountain Lion economies, now among the fastest growing in the nation thanks to reasonable prices, growing high-tech economies, good weather or natural beauty, and relatively low state and local taxes. Like many western settlements, Boise's development since the mid-1800s involved natural resources (in its case gold), the arrival of railroads and heavy federal investment in military facilities, dams and reservoirs. A big step toward modernization came in the 1970s when Silicon Valley's Hewlett-Packard set up a Boise office. It remains—along with the local semicon firm Micron—a major area employer. Retailers like Walmart and Costco are big employers. So are Wells Fargo and the local power company. Less important is government employment despite being the state capital. That said, the government-run Boise State University is huge, enrolling more than 20,000 students and employing 3,500 workers. Simply put, the arrival of people and money from California are fueling a mountain economy boom, none more dynamic than the one in Boise. That means the job market is better in Boise now than it was even pre-crisis, something very much *not* the case nationwide. Now, Amazon—already a big employer—is adding lots of Boise jobs. Unfortunately, this also means a housing crisis, not to mention more traffic and other irritants associated with rapid expansion. A good tradeoff? Many Americans seem to think so.

FRANKLIN COUNTY, NEW YORK

September 2021

It shares a name with the world's richest and most powerful city. But in the farthest northern reaches of New York state, the world looks a whole lot different. In Franklin County, New York, which borders Canada, the worries don't involve soaring rents or unreliable subway service. There, the worries are more typical of troubled rural America, where populations are shrinking and economies struggling to create good jobs. Indeed, Franklin County's population dropped by 3% during the 2010s, even as the U.S. population grew 6%. In 2015, the aluminum maker Alcoa closed a nearby plant that extinguished about 500 jobs from the area. In 2017, the now-famous drug giant Pfizer closed a plant, costing the region 120 jobs. The county is heavily dependent on the public sector, which accounts for more than half of total employment. Particularly important are several correctional facilities (that's another term for prisons). Even in this sector though, job opportunities have diminished, with one prison closing in 2014. Statistics on the county's roughly 50,000 people make the region's difficulties clear. Median household income is just $50,000, versus $63,000 nationally. The poverty rate is 18%, versus 11% nationally. Unemployment rates were above the national average before Covid. So was the prevalence of residents collecting disability insurance. According to 2017 data from Franklin County's economic development plan, the percentage of 16-to-19-year-olds not in school, not graduated and not employed was twice as high than the national rate. Another challenge is geography. Fort Covington, which touches the Canadian border in the northernmost area of the county, is nearly 400 miles from New York City. Even Albany and Syracuse are hours away by car. Rural areas are gaining an advantage in the new world of remote working but only if broadband internet connections are fast and reliable—in Franklin County, that's a problem. The area's population, furthermore, is spread across a vast area, featuring the largest town Malone but also the Saranac Lake and Tupper Lake regions. The cold winters don't help either—it's the Sun Belt where people are moving, starting companies and taking jobs. Where *do* people in Franklin County work, besides correctional facilities? The largest private employer (with about 900 jobs) is the Akwesasne Casino on the Mohawk reservation. Native Americans, still 8% of the county's population today, have a long history in the area. Non-Hispanic Whites, meanwhile, account for 82% of the population, with foreign born residents just 3%. But back to employment, the health and education sectors are (welcome to 2021 America) important, accounting for 35% and 13% of all county jobs, respectively. Naturally, trade with Canada is important—Montreal is less than a two-hour drive from Malone. But the border was closed for an extended period due to Covid. That hurt. Though disadvantaged by geography, the area's lakes and mountains attract a good number of tourists, including skiers during winter. Lake Placid, once the site of the Winter Olympics, lies just south of the county. Logging was once a much larger industry in upstate New York, before the days of foreign competition, product substitution, tougher environmental standards and skilled worker shortages. But what's left of logging today is benefitting from a strong national market for homebuilding. Just an hour away in Plattsburgh is an airport with lots of low-fare flights. Not far west is the water port of Ogdensburg, an important trading gateway on the St. Lawrence River. Franklin County could benefit if only it could get a rail link to the port, which would also connect with the major CSX freight rail line to Syracuse and beyond. One of the area's biggest draws, meanwhile, is some of the cheapest electricity rates anywhere in the country, supported by abundant hydro and other clean power. Unfortunately, the current power grid doesn't support the ability to export surplus power to New York City. But it does offer power-hungry businesses, including cryptocurrency miners and data storage operators, an important advantage. Development officials also trumpet the county's affordable housing and surplus labor at a time of severe shortages. This includes many experienced military veterans, correctional officers and former employees of Alcoa and Pfizer. The correctional officers, interestingly, also happen to retire at an early age on average, and many might be interested in pursuing second careers. Is this enough? To be frank about Franklin, the county is part of forgotten America, worlds away from the nation's economic engines and migratory magnets. But it's not without economic assets, cheap power most intriguing among them.

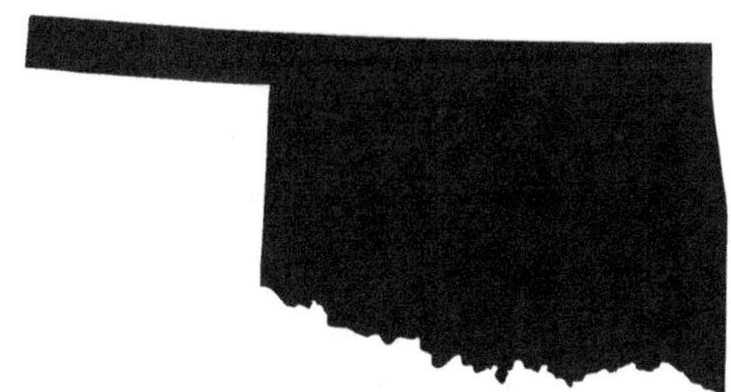

OKLAHOMA CITY, OKLAHOMA

October 2021

Looking for a job? You might want to head for Oklahoma. In August 2021, the state's capital—Oklahoma City—had the lowest jobless rate in the nation among metro areas with more than 1m people. A month earlier, it ranked number two, behind only Salt Lake City. What's behind Oklahoma City's economic success? Start with the energy sector, now roaring back after a dramatic fall at the onset of the Covid crisis. Since the early 1900s, oil and gas have shaped the Oklahoman economy. Tulsa was once called the "oil capital of the world." Cushing, an hour's drive northeast of Oklahoma City, is today a hub for crude oil pipelines, and home to about 15% of all U.S. commercial storage capacity. Oklahoma City itself is home to Devon Energy, a big oil company that recently got bigger by merging with Tulsa's WPX. In 2020, Oklahoma ranked number four among U.S. states for crude oil and natural gas production, according to the U.S. Energy Information Administration. The annual value of its production last year: More than $3b, says Oklahoma's Historical Society. Sure enough, when oil prices collapsed in the 1980s and 1990s, Oklahoma City suffered. The year 1995 was a symbolic low point, darkened by a major act of domestic terrorism in the city's downtown. The first 15 years of the 2000s, however, brought a surge in people, jobs and oil money, not to mention heavy investment in downtown amenities—including professional sports franchises—that made the city a regional tourist draw. Things got tough again after the oil crash of the mid 2010s, slowing the pace of population growth. But still, the number of people in the metro area grew 12% during the decade, making it the nation's 42nd largest by 2020. Oil and gas, however, don't explain everything. The city's aerospace sector is another reason Oklahoma City's job market is so hot right now. The Tinker Air Force base alone employs about 24,000 people. The Federal Aviation Administration (FAA) employs another 7,000. Boeing, Pratt & Whitney and Northrup Grumman, all big defense contractors, are big employers. So are lesser-known military aerospace manufacturers like Kratos and Valkyrie, both producers of pilotless drones. Oklahoma City's largest employer is the state government, always a solid and stable source of well-paid jobs for a city. The University of Oklahoma in nearby Norman is another anchor for the local job market. Same for hospitals and other health care facilities. Aside from Devon Energy, companies headquartered in the city include the retailers Hobby Lobby and Love's, the fast-food chain Sonic and the fast-growing payroll software firm Paycom. In January, the city opened a $288m convention center, creating hundreds of new jobs. The new First Americans Museum opened just last month, honoring Oklahoma's 39 distinct tribal nations (many forcibly moved there in the 19th century). Another lure for jobseekers is the city's relatively low housing prices. Like practically everywhere else during the pandemic, home prices have increased, in Oklahoma's City's case by 14% in the past year, according to the Federal Housing Finance Agency (FHFA). But that's one of the smallest gains among all big metro areas—Boise's housing prices are up 41%. Jeff Seymour and Eric Long, both with the Greater Oklahoma City Chamber of Commerce, also attribute the economy's recent success to a legacy of productive planning and cooperation between public and private leaders, along with successful investment of sales tax dollars. Taking a more expansive geographic view, Oklahoma City is just three hours by car from the booming Dallas-Fort Worth Metroplex, with the space in between fast filling up with people and homes. The entire Interstate-35 corridor in fact, is by some measures the fastest growing "mega-politan" region, to use a term favored by some demographers. As truckers and railroaders know, I-35 is one of North America's busiest highways for freight transport, stretching from the Great Lakes port of Duluth to the busy U.S.-Mexican border town of Laredo, with metros like Minneapolis, Des Moines, Kansas City, Wichita, Oklahoma City, Dallas-Fort Worth, Austin and San Antonio along the way. Does all this position Oklahoma City to be the next Austin in terms of economic superstardom? Well, the one big thing still missing is a large-scale tech sector—much of Austin's spectacular rise is thanks to companies like Dell, Apple, Tesla, IBM and Korea's Samsung. Oklahoma City's energy sector exposure, meanwhile, makes it still vulnerable to oil price slumps, not to mention the "great transition" to renewable energy. Alas, not every city can be Austin. But nor can every city have the best unemployment rate in the country. That distinction—right now—belongs to Oklahoma City.

PITTSBURGH, PENNSYLVANIA

October 2021

A rust belt relic? Or a high-tech all-star? Today, Silicon Valley is the symbol of America's information-age prowess. A century ago, it was Pittsburgh that symbolized the nation's economic power, then expressed through industrial might. As late as 1910, the City of Steel was America's sixth largest, behind only New York, Chicago, Philadelphia, Boston and St. Louis. Its steel proved essential to building the railroads, skyscrapers and military machinery that shaped much of the country's history. Few cities were home to as many major corporations—Alcoa, Gulf Oil, H.J. Heinz, Mellon Bank, Westinghouse… and most famously, U.S. Steel. But then came the plunge. As Pittsburgh's steel industry gradually withered, so did its economic fortunes. Between 1910 and 2000, the U.S. population increased threefold, notes Pittsburgh Quarterly, but Allegheny County (home to Pittsburgh) lost 9% of its residents. The decline, alas, continues today. During the 2010s, Pittsburgh's population shrank another 2%, most among the country's top 50 metros, save Puerto Rico's capital San Juan. Its contraction has been more akin to smaller metros emblematic of post-industrial decline, like Syracuse, Toledo, Scranton and Youngstown. In the 2020 census,

Pittsburgh's 2.4m people ranked 27th nationwide among all U.S. metros, this after still ranking in the top 10 as late as 1970—and in the top 20 as late as 1990. The early 1980s marked the city's low point. Unemployment reached 17% as the region lost 133,000 manufacturing jobs between 1979 and 1987, the Pittsburgh Post-Gazette reported. Between 2002 and 2005, according to the Department of Housing and Urban Development (HUD), the manufacturing sector shed an average of 5,800 jobs per year, with another 2,400 losses in the closely related transportation and utilities sectors. Early in the new century, Pittsburgh lost its status as a major passenger airline hub. When the 2008 recession hit, the region lost another 28,000 jobs, nearly 10,000 of them in manufacturing. Japan's Sony, to give just one example, closed its last remaining U.S. television manufacturing plant in Pittsburgh that year, laying off 560 employees. As mentioned, population continued to shrink throughout the 2010s, ranking number one among metros for the highest net migration outflow to other states. Tellingly, the largest number of residents left for Tampa, many of them retirees. HUD data shows that more than a quarter of migrants fleeing out of state were older than 65. But even with so many seniors leaving, a full fifth of Pittsburgh's residents today are over 65, compared to 17% nationwide. Pittsburgh, in other words, is a metaphor for U.S. metros facing the triple challenge of deindustrialization, population loss and aging demographics. But guess what? That's only half the story, and a misleading half. Pittsburgh—cue the cheerful music—is also a metaphor for U.S. metros achieving remarkable success in meeting many of these challenges. No, the steel mills aren't coming back. And yes, population decline remains a concern. But in an age when luring technology companies is the economic development equivalent of scoring touchdowns, then Pittsburgh is Ben Roethlisberger in his prime (substitute the name Terry Bradshaw if you'd like). Google, Facebook, Uber and Zoom are a few of the companies with major offices in the area, enticed by Carnegie-Mellon University's world-class computer science program. The school also benefits from government-funded research focused on artificial intelligence and robotics, making Pittsburgh a leader in both fields. The city is on the front lines of autonomous vehicle development, with several leading companies in the field choosing Pittsburgh as their corporate headquarters.

Carnegie-Mellon is of course a big employer itself, as are the University of Pittsburgh and Duquesne University. Education and health care, which have replaced manufacturing as the largest providers of jobs throughout much of America, now employs 22% of all workers in the Pittsburgh metro, up from 17% two decades ago. Health care, of course, includes everything from a hospital custodian to highly paid doctors and medical researchers, and Pittsburgh has an abundance of the latter. University of Pittsburgh Medical Center and Highmark Healthcare are the area's two largest employers, followed by the University of Pittsburgh. Next is PNC, the country's fifth largest bank and a reason (along with BNY Mellon's presence) why Pittsburgh is also a major financial center. And adding to the diversification, it's a major center for the oil and gas industry too. The surrounding Marcellus Formation is the largest source of natural gas in the U.S. and the site of a drilling boom that began in 2007 as fracking technology transformed the industry. Europe's Royal Dutch Shell will soon complete a $6b petrochemical plant on the banks of the Ohio River, turning low-cost ethane from shale gas into polyethylene, a kind of plastic used in everything from food packaging to auto parts. Interestingly, Shell says more than 70% of North American polyethylene customers are within a 700-mile radius of Pittsburgh, giving the new plant an advantage over more distant Gulf Coast operators. This geographical advantage, incidentally, also makes Pittsburgh a growing logistics hub for companies like Amazon. Some 6,000 construction workers are involved in the Shell project, which will employ about 600 people when completed. What more to say about Pittsburgh's renaissance? Its picturesque downtown, with sports venues and spectacular bridges, are a draw to millennials. Living costs are relatively low. Severe air pollution is no longer the problem it was during steel's heyday. And the city has on multiple occasions played host to major international conferences, including the 2009 G20 Summit (right in the middle of the global financial crisis) and last month's U.S.-EU Trade and Technology Council. Pittsburgh, in sum, is Exhibit A in America's shift from an industrial economy centered on making physical stuff to one much more characterized by providing services to people, most importantly health care and education services. The transition hasn't been easy, and challenges remain, most importantly demographic challenges (that shrinking population base). But Pittsburgh is nevertheless a case study in success, with a high-tech knowledge economy that all cities crave. Maybe it's time to change the name of the Pittsburgh Steelers. The "Pittsburgh Artificial Intelligence Algorithms?" With a self-driving car logo on their helmets? You know what? Let's keep them the Steelers.

37

THE VILLAGES, FLORIDA

October 2021

It's the dream of every child: To visit Mickey, Donald, Goofy and Pluto in Orlando. But there's a different group of people who dream of central Florida—of living there, in fact. Just an hour north of Disney's Magic Kingdom is a kingdom of sorts where children aren't welcome—as residents, anyway. It's a giant retirement community called The Villages, spread across three Florida counties. And guess what? It was America's fastest growing metro area during the 2010s. It kind of makes sense—The U.S. population is rapidly aging, with retiring Baby Boomers creating a senior bulge. The research group PRB projects the number of Americans aged 65 and older to increase from 54m in 2019 (16% of the total population) to nearly double that by 2060 (23% of the total population). That's a future with nearly one out of every four people old enough to qualify for benefits like Social Security pensions and Medicare, implying heavy fiscal pressure on these programs. The demographic shift, furthermore, could have profound effects on the labor market, and on the types of products and services consumed. Actually, the effects are already visible—just look at the huge expansion of the health care sector even since 2000, when just 12% of the U.S. population was 65-plus (it was 11% in 1980). One thing about demographic trends: You can see them coming in advance. At least one visionary real estate developer certainly did. H. Gary Morse, born in Chicago, moved to central Florida in 1983, according to his Wikipedia bio, after taking control of his father's business selling vacant Florida lots to mobile homeowners. Recognizing the future market for retirees seeking sunshine, leisure activities, good health care facilities and affordable living, he began building homes with access to community restaurants, pools, golf courses and other amenities. Sure enough, the retirees came, and Morse (now deceased) became a billionaire. Today, The Villages consists of 78 separate communities, where people get around in golf carts and—in most of the communities anyway—residents must be at least 55 years old. Homebuilders benefit from a special Florida legal arrangement called Community Development Districts (CDDs), of which there are 17 within The Villages. CDDs essentially give property developers the right to finance their investments by issuing tax-privileged bonds, like a local government or school district. More than 130,000 people (98% of them White) now reside in the metro area, up some 40% in the past decade. The vast majority are seniors. But then who provides the services they need? According to a Tampa Times report earlier this month, roughly 15,000 employees work in The Villages, most of them younger than 55. More are moving in to reduce their commutes, as they're allowed to do according to a Florida law that permits up to 20% of residents in an age-restricted retirement community to be under 55. There's otherwise some small-scale agriculture and manufacturing in the region. But the economy is first and foremost about real estate development for retirees, and providing these retirees services, from serving food to selling golf carts to preforming surgery. As one resident quoted in the Tampa Times article said: "It's Disneyworld for adults here."

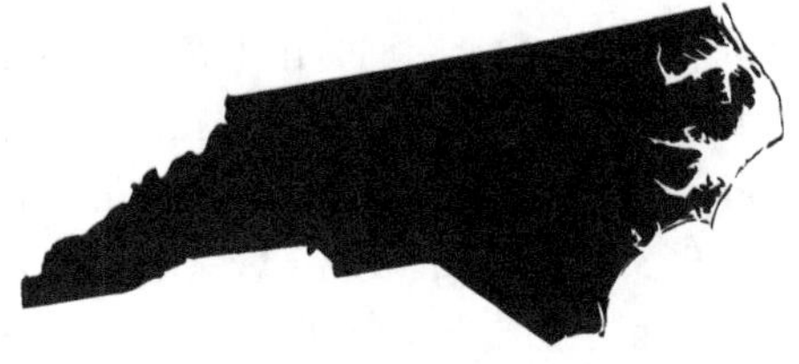

38

CHARLOTTE, NORTH CAROLINA

October 2021

There's an old joke in the airline industry: When you die and go to heaven, you'll have to make a stop in Atlanta. That's Atlanta, the busiest airport in the world. But you might make the same joke about Charlotte, America's sixth busiest airport despite being its 22nd largest metro. Just four hours by road northeast of Atlanta, North Carolina's largest city enjoys much of the same geographic advantage for air transport, situated along the path between many of the nation's busiest traffic flows, including almost everything into and out of Florida. Amid the demand devastation of 2020, Charlotte—without much international exposure—saw the smallest y/y decline in traffic of any major U.S. airline hub. That enabled it to achieve its number six ranking nationwide. But even pre-crisis, in 2019, it was the country's 11th busiest airport, punching far above its weight. It also happens to be among the world's most profitable airline hubs, in its case dominated by American Airlines (which employs more than 10,000 people in the region). Charlotte's geography, however, doesn't just work well for airlines. It works well for trucking too, with a strong highway network allowing easy access to more than half of America's population—indeed, that's how many people live within a 650-mile radius. This includes Washington, New York and much of Florida. It also includes Detroit and the many auto factories across the Southeast. Sure enough, Charlotte now has an auto-cluster of its own, which includes a Daimler factory producing trucks. The area's distribution benefits also make it a hot spot for retailers, including Amazon and several major supermarket chains. Charlotte is home to Lowe's, the giant home improvement retailer, along with non-retailers like Duke Energy and the hospital network Atrium. It's a big sports town too, with NASCAR, the Hornets and the Panthers (but no Major League Baseball team, at least not yet). UNC Charlotte enrolls 30,000 students. In addition, the city is in a relatively low-cost area of the eastern seaboard, and one with sunny weather. No wonder why the Charlotte metro population spiked 17% during the 2010s. According to the Charlotte Regional Business Alliance, the area's job count is down by just 3.1% from its pre-pandemic level, compared to a 4.4% decline nationally. Since Q2 2020, the Alliance notes, foreign-owned firms have announced more than $600m in new capital investments, led by the Korean owner of Bobcat construction equipment. But there's something else—something that distinguishes Charlotte from even its bigger neighbor Atlanta. The city, surprisingly, is one of America's top banking centers, behind only New York City and San Francisco in total deposits. Like so many U.S. cities, Charlotte owes its early development to the arrival of railroads, in its case just before the Civil War. The financial sector later grew as the city needed capital to finance its emergence as a hub for cotton and textile manufacturing, much of it migrating from New England where labor costs were higher. This gave rise to the North Carolina National Bank (NCNB), created through a merger in the 1950s. As the Charlotte Museum of History explains, NCNB benefitted from a 1985 state law—the Southeastern Regional Banking Compact—which allowed North Carolina banks to own branches in other states but disallowed northern banks from entering North Carolina. As the Museum explains: "This act of protectionism allowed NCNB to continue expansion with little fear of acquisition by an outside bank." And so, NCNB, which changed its name to NationsBank, grew and grew, with one merger after another. In 1998, it bought San Francisco-based Bank of America and—while keeping its headquarters in Charlotte—kept the BOA name. All the while, another North Carolina-based bank called Wachovia engaged in a similar acquisition-fueled growth spree. Unfortunately, it got caught up in the sub-prime mortgage mess of the mid-2000s, leading to its near-collapse and eventual takeover by San Francisco's Wells Fargo, which nevertheless maintained Charlotte as its eastern headquarters. More recently, when Winston-Salem's BB&T decided to merge with Atlanta's SunTrust, they selected Charlotte as their new home. Today, Charlotte's banking talent makes it a top site for fintech companies, including USAA, Lending Tree and Credit Karma. The banks, to be sure, greatly value the abundant air service Charlotte offers. In fact, Honeywell, known for its aerospace technology, recently moved its headquarters to a site adjacent to the airport, citing its convenience as a major reason for its decision (it moved from New Jersey). One thing Charlotte is not: A state capital, like Atlanta or Nashville. It's not a big tourist draw either. Its *intercontinental* air service is limited. But judging from the recent past, Charlotte's future nonetheless appears bright. You can bank on it.

PROVO, UTAH

November 2021

I f the job market were a sport, Utah would have a Silver Medal. Only 2.4% of its workforce is unemployed, best in the nation save Nebraska (the Cornhusker state takes the Gold at 2.0%). Believe it or not, Utah's current unemployment rate is lower *now* than it was pre-Covid! Not even Nebraska can say that (Only Utah and Idaho can). Something's going very right about Utah's economy, and you can see it in a place like Provo. That's the home of Brigham Young University (BYU), one of the largest private universities in the U.S. based on undergraduate enrollment. The school's 34,000 students, combined with those studying at nearby Utah Valley University, accounted for 11% of Provo's population pre-Covid, according to the HUD's latest housing market analysis. BYU is run by The Church of Jesus Christ of Latter-day Saints, whose adherents settled in Utah during the 19th century, fleeing persecution. Highly centralized, the Church plays a large role in Provo's economy, not just through BYU but also institutions like a major training center for Latter-day Saints missionaries. Likewise critical to Provo's economy is nearby Salt Lake City, with its many jobs within commuting distance. The Church itself employs nearly 10,000 people in Salt

Lake. The state government is another big employer (Salt Lake is Utah's state capital). Large medical facilities, a major Delta and UPS air hub and a vibrant financial sector headed by Zions Bank underpin the job market as well—Salt Lake is home to the largest Goldman Sachs office in the U.S. outside of New York. But for those in Provo who'd rather not commute north, good news: The local economy is buzzing as well. The two universities alone employ around 25,000 people. There's the Utah Valley medical center. Retailers like Walmart provide lots of jobs. The largest non-education, private-sector employer in the area is Vivant, a provider of solar power. Based on HUD data, the Provo-Orem metro area, distinct from Salt Lake City, employed 7,400 software publishers and data processing analysts in 2018. This was up from 4,500 in 2010, and consistent with the meteoric rise in the area's population. Few places grew as quickly during the 2010s—population increased 22%, with annual job growth averaging 5%. Since 2011, according to the HUD's housing market report, Provo had 87,000 more jobs in 2018 than it did in 2011, an increase of nearly 50%. Some came for the education. Others for the education jobs. Still others came for the area's natural beauty and outdoor recreation. Provo, a top skiing destination, hosted part of the 2002 Winter Olympics. It's also near the Sundance Resort, home to the famed Sundance Film Festival. Provo, meanwhile, is a major breeding ground for technology startups, giving the region its "Silicon Slopes" nickname. The Milken Institute, which looks at criteria like job creation, wage gains and tech-prowess to rank the economic strength of metro areas, named Provo number one on its list last year, ahead of some 400 other places. Qualtrics, NuSkin, Caselle and Imagine Learning are the names of some local companies. The city, to be sure, has a high degree of college graduates. It also has the highest birthrate of any U.S. metro area, averaging 7.3 children per 1,000 residents. That makes it a young city, but also one with many retirees and remote workers. The Rocky Mountain region perhaps fared better than any other during America's struggle with Covid. Even tourism held up relatively well—in July, just before the Delta variant emerged, Salt Lake's airport was just 1% off its 2019 passenger counts. Provo has its own little airport, which will get a new terminal next year. With ultra-fast growth, naturally, comes problems, including higher housing prices, more traffic and complaints of pollution. The problems are far worse, though, for places that shrink. Provo has come a long way since the railroad first came to town in the 1870s. Today, it's an economic Gold Medalist.

40

BOONE COUNTY, WEST VIRGINIA

November 2021

You just read about Provo, Utah, whose economy is prospering thanks to an educated workforce, a fast-growing population, an ecosystem of finance and tech talent, an influx of retirees and remote workers, proximity to a booming city (Salt Lake), a vibrant tourist sector, good broadband infrastructure and a large anchor employer, in its case Brigham Young University. Boone County, West Virginia, sadly, has none of these. There, an economy that once thrived thanks to a single commodity—coal—now struggles to survive as coal's usefulness wanes. Located in the state's southwest amid the Appalachian plateau, Boone has 13% fewer residents now than it did in 2010. That's on par with the decline in Puerto Rico, an economy with its own set of enormous challenges. In Boone, more than a fifth of all residents are over 65. Less than 1% are foreign born (A full 98% of the population is White). And fewer than one in ten people have a college degree (compared to one in three nationally). The disturbing data doesn't end there. A fifth of all Boone County residents are classified as having a disability. As the national economy frets about a worryingly low 63% worker participation rate, the rate in Boone County is just 40%. In the nearby Huntington metro area, federal HUD statistics show that roughly one in three residents say they've been diagnosed with depression—that's the highest rate nationwide. Even closer than Huntington is the state capital Charleston, where at least some well-paid government and health care jobs are available. But even here, sharp population declines, opioid addiction, disappearing chemical production and widespread poverty cast a dark shadow. Speaking of the opioid tragedy, the area's Regional Intergovernmental Council, citing a study by the American Enterprise Institute, says the epidemic is costing Boone County's economy an estimated $206.5 million a year, the highest per-capita burden of any county in the U.S. A coal mining job, if you can get one, pays well, even today. But in Boone County, just two mining companies—Blackhawk and Alpha— are left following the closure of multiple mines since coal's heyday in the 1950s. Blackhawk and Alpha are still, sure enough, the county's top two private sector employers. Statewide, coal production dropped 31% from 2011 to 2019, according to Southerly. And just last year, as the pandemic ravaged demand for power and steel, coal sector employment in West Virginia declined 18%, to roughly 11,000 (once upon a time the figure topped 100,000). Boone County, with just 13 active coal mines left, finds itself in a cycle of spiraling decline: Fewer jobs and coal revenue mean less income and fewer people. Fewer people means a shrinking tax base. A shrinking tax base means less money for public services, like schools, police protection and hospitals. Setting aside the starkly different racial demographics, the impact of lost coal jobs on Boone County looks much like the impact of lost steel jobs in another city profiled earlier in this book: Gary, Indiana. Critical to keeping things together are federal programs like Social Security and Medicaid. Boone County will now gain federal funding for broadband development, a key feature of the infrastructure bill passed in Washington last week. Helpfully, coal is currently experiencing a sharp if likely brief revival, with prices for natural gas (a competing source of electricity generation) soaring. But this won't make up for even the setbacks of the Covid crisis, let alone the setbacks of coal's multi-decade decline. In Boone County, incidentally, just 45% of eligible residents are fully vaccinated against Covid. West Virginia, meanwhile, was President

Trump's strongest state in the 2020 election, securing 69% of the vote. He took 73% in Boone County. But don't jump to conclusions when it comes to politics: President Obama won the state in 2008.

41

DES MOINES, IOWA

November 2021

Corn? Soybeans? Hogs? Yep, that's Iowa. But financial services? Iowa is indeed an agricultural powerhouse, ranking second behind California in the value of its farm output. But in the state capital Des Moines, you'll more likely encounter someone measuring risk than harvesting crops. Des Moines is home to more than 70 insurance companies, not to mention the industry's Global Insurance Symposium held each year. Principal Financial and Nationwide are the two largest insurance firms in the area. The largest private-sector employer is Wells Fargo, which houses its giant home mortgage business in Des Moines, employing nearly 15,000 locals. According to the Census, no major metro area in the country has a higher concentration of workers in financial services. The category accounts for a full 15% of all nonfarm payroll jobs, higher than even New York City's 11%. Just north of the city (in Ames) is Iowa State University, which offers actuarial science degrees to aspiring insurance professionals. Drake University in downtown Des Moines offers these as well. Combined with lots of jobs in state government, local government, education and health care, the financial service sector forms the backbone of a strong Des Moines labor market, currently sporting an unemployment rate of just 2.9%. The national rate is 4.6%. Agriculture certainly matters. In fact, many of the city's insurance firms were founded in the 19th century, offering risk mitigation to farmers. Nationwide, as it happens, used to be called Farm Bureau Mutual. Other big employers in the Des Moines metro include manufacturers like Vermeer, which sells various agriculture, construction and mining equipment. Tractor maker John Deere, though based in Illinois, has its customer financing arm in Des Moines. Rockwell Collins, now part of Raytheon has a big presence too. The Greater Des Moines Partnership, an economic development group, ranks Hy-Vee, a supermarket chain, as the metro area's fourth largest private-sector employer after Wells Fargo, UnityPoint Hospital and Principal. A broader geography encompassing 16 surrounding counties forms what's called the Cultivation Corridor, home to many bioscience and biotechnology ventures focusing on improving agricultural productivity. Thanks to an abundance of clean and renewable wind power, Des Moines has become a leading site for energy-hungry data centers; Apple, Facebook and Microsoft all have data centers there. So does Amazon, which also has a distribution center and—in total—employs about 3,500 locals. Then there's JBS, a Brazilian meat producer that operates a large pork processing plant northeast of Des Moines, staffed mostly by immigrants from Latin America, eastern Europe and Southeast Asia (notably Myanmar). Also part of the plant's 2,300-member workforce are numerous refugees from the East African country Sudan. Sure enough, 8% of the Des Moines metro population is now foreign born, in a state that's 95% U.S.-born. Overall, it ranks just 84th in the country by population, too small to have a large airline hub or a major league sports franchise. It's growing though, with 15% more people now than in 2010. That makes it one of the fastest growing midwestern metros, with Minneapolis, Omaha, Kansas City and St. Louis all growing more slowly during the 2010s. Omaha is the closest "big" city geographically, roughly two hours away by car. Minneapolis and Kansas City are more like three-to-four hours and Chicago closer to five. What else accounts for the impressive population growth besides a healthy job market? According to Moody's Analytics, the cost of doing business in Des Moines is 13% below the national average. The cost of housing is manageable too.

Brian Crowe, executive VP of economic development for the Greater Des Moines Partnership, highlights investments in downtown cultural amenities to draw more talented professionals. He also trumpets the area's potential to help the world transition to a carbon-free economy: "We can lead in the Green Revolution." Des Moines does face environmental risks, including floods. In 2016, it experienced what was deemed the costliest thunderstorm in U.S. history. The good news about future risks? Residents won't have to look far for insurance.

(42)

BALTIMORE, MARYLAND

November 2021

There's a familiar story in America's Northeast Corridor, a stretch of territory that links Boston in the north with Washington, DC in the south. It was the original epicenter of America's economy when America was still a colony of Britain. Indeed, the Northeast Corridor's Big Five cities (minus Washington) all date to colonial times. Some three centuries later, in 2021, all have giant economies, highly educated populations and world-class universities and medical facilities. Several have major seaports. Some are global tourist attractions. One (Washington) is the nation's political capital. Another (New York) is the nation's financial capital. Still another (Boston) is a global center of bioscience. All five, moreover, have rings of extremely wealthy suburbs surrounding their city centers. Not all five, however, have had the same success reviving their city centers after all experienced de-industrialization and mass exodus of middle class mostly White families to the suburbs. All five cities were at some point on their knees: New York for its part faced an epic fiscal crisis in the 1970s. Washington was once called the murder capital of America. When Massachusetts governor Mike Dukakis ran for President in 1988, one of the big campaign issues was just how filthy Boston Harbor had become. New York, alas, recaptured its economic glory with help from finance, real estate, media and tourism. Boston did the same with help from IT, education and biomedicine. Washington thrived as the Federal government (along with defense contractors) greatly expanded. Philadelphia's city center, on the other hand, even as its suburbs prospered, remained stuck with very high rates of poverty, not unlike city centers of the de-industrialized Midwest (i.e., Detroit and Cleveland). Of the five Northeast Corridor cities, there's one not yet mentioned, which perhaps speaks to its relative economic weakness. It's Baltimore, whose story sadly reads more like Philadelphia than the others. But even worse. The city, the only one in Maryland not part of a county (Baltimore *county* is a separate political entity), certainly has its wealthy surrounding counties. Howard County, for example, has a median household income of $122,000. The wider Baltimore metro area, with almost 3m people, is the country's 21st largest, similar in population to the Charlotte or St. Louis metros. Its 3% growth during the 2010s was slow, but the suburbs grew more or less on pace with its northeastern peers. Southeast of downtown, on the Chesapeake Bay, is Baltimore's vibrant seaport, incidentally the busiest nationwide for auto exports and imports. Amazon alone has five warehouses around the port, which is well-positioned for e-commerce. Baltimore sits right along Amtrak's busy northeast rail corridor and Interstate 95. Airport access is excellent too, with Baltimore-Washington International airport (BWI) one of Southwest's largest bases. The metro area's largest employer though, is the Federal Government, and more specifically Fort George Meade, with about 54,000 workers. Another military facility, Aberdeen Proving Ground, employs about 21,000. And both facilities grew a lot after 2005, when various bases elsewhere in the country were shuttered to cut costs. Greater Baltimore is also home to the headquarters of the National Security Agency, the Social Security Administration, the Center for Medicaid & Medicare Services and about 60 other federal agencies and research labs. Notable companies in the region include Northrop Grumman (defense), Under Armour (apparel), Exelon (energy) and Legg Mason (finance). Another giant piece of the area economy: Johns Hopkins University and Hospital, the country's largest recipients of federal academic research dollars and together responsible for about 50,000 jobs. The University of Maryland has a large Baltimore medical facility as well. Together, education and health account for about 20% of all area jobs. Add government and the trade/transportation/utility sector and you surpass 50%. The next largest sector is leisure and here, Baltimore's inner core has a pretty good story to tell. The Inner Harbor, specifically, became a celebrated example of post-industrial waterfront redevelopment, attracting millions of tourists and convention goers. The aquarium is popular. So are the restaurants (crabcakes!) and sports stadiums. Even before the pandemic, though, the tourism sector was slowing, in part due to rising crime. In 2019, the New York Times and ProPublica jointly ran an article entitled "The Tragedy of Baltimore, Inside the Crackup of an American City." One sentence captures the gist: "In 2017, it recorded 342 murders—its highest per-capita rate ever, more than double Chicago's, far higher than any other city of 500,000 or more residents and, astonishingly, a larger absolute number of killings than in New York, a city 14 times as populous." As HUD data show, Baltimore city was losing more than 4,000 people a year in the late 2010s, following net in-migration of more than 4,000 between 2010 and 2015, when younger, more educated and affluent people began trickling in. As of Jan. 1, 2021, the city's population was about 586,000, down from a peak of 950,000 in 1950. According to a history published by the city's government, Baltimore proper was already losing 10,000 people during the 1950s, followed by a 35,000-person loss in the 1960s. Most who could—but not many African Americans who largely couldn't—left for the suburbs, and with them went companies, jobs, stores and federal investment, most importantly in highways and home loans. Older, multi-story brick factories were vacated, replaced by suburban industrial parks with quick access to new highways. Inner city neighborhoods and shopping districts crumbled. Thousands of homes and shops were demolished to make way for expressways and public housing projects. This familiar pattern contributed to many of the social ills of contemporary urban America. But as mentioned, some cities like New York, Washington and Boston were able to revive their downtowns in recent decades. Baltimore didn't, beyond the Inner Harbor area anyway. Last week, the Baltimore Sun reported the city's 300th homicide in 2021, reaching that total for the seventh straight year. The Bureau of Labor Statistics, incidentally, said the Baltimore metro area's 5.3% unemployment rate in September was the least improved y/y of any large metro in the country. The Baltimore City school district's budget problems didn't help—it was forced to lay off 400 workers in late 2020. Locals with longer memories will recall 2005, when General Motors closed a van assembly plant in the city. Enrollment at local colleges and universities, meanwhile, operating in the shadow of Johns Hopkins, has been steadily declining for the past 9 years. But there's hope. The new Infrastructure Investment and Jobs Act will direct new funds to boost Baltimore's economy, notably via road and rail projects. Its port is one of the few still operating smoothly at a time of great supply chain disruptions. President Biden, in fact, chose the Port of Baltimore as a venue to tout his new infrastructure bill. Baltimore is certainly in a good place geographically, with plenty of wealth, talent and resources within its metro area borders. It's shown the world once how it can revive a part of the inner city. But in 2021, too many of its neighborhoods lack economic opportunity, for reasons that touch difficult issues like race relations and law enforcement. Can Baltimore make a comeback?

YUMA, ARIZONA

November 2021

There aren't too many places in the world wealthier than San Diego. There aren't too many places growing faster than Phoenix. But in between is mostly nothingness, just vast stretches of desert, especially on the Arizona side. There is, however, a city called Yuma. It's not large—roughly 200,000 people in its Census area. It's certainly not rich—median household incomes are almost $20,000 less than the national average. But it is growing—Yuma metro's population increased nearly 9% during the 2010s. Why are people moving to Yuma? As it turns out, for several good reasons. Americans first started passing through the area during the California gold rush of 1849, long before Arizona was even a state (that didn't happen until 1912). Yuma happened to be a good place to cross the Colorado River. The Laguna dam just north of Yuma would be the first one built on the Colorado. Later, during the Depression, desperate farmers from the drought-stricken Great Plains came through hoping to land jobs in California's fertile Central Valley. Many were turned away by California state police, thereafter forced to settle in Yuma. A decade later, during World War II, Yuma's primitive economy evolved into something more substantial when it became an important outpost for military training and weapons testing. Sure enough, it retains that role today, with federal defense spending a critical pillar of the contemporary Yuma economy. The Yuma Proving Ground, a testing facility for drones and other weapons, generates more than $1.1b in economic activity, the city's government estimates. The U.S. Marine Corp., meanwhile, operates an aviation training facility generating more than $600m in activity. There is one sector, however, that's even more central to the economy: Agriculture. Yuma produces some 90% of America's supply of winter vegetables (i.e., lettuce and broccoli) aided by water irrigated from the Colorado River). More recently, Yuma has attracted lower-income retirees seeking winter sunshine and affordable homes. The Greater Yuma Economic Development Corp. (GYEDC), charged with attracting new businesses to the area, highlights the importance of logistics, warehousing and distribution. Food processing is another major sector, as is aerospace thanks to synergies with all the military activity. Yuma now wants to leverage its vast unoccupied airspace and favorable weather to develop a spaceport for commercial rocket launches. The GYEDC, meanwhile, touts a "reasonable" regulatory environment, low housing costs and a bilingual workforce ideal for services like call centers (Allstate Insurance has one in the area). Aside from the military, the local school district, the county government and the local hospital, the largest employer in Yuma is a farmer-owned company called Date Pac, which as the name suggests, produces, packages and distributes dates. Several Native tribal governments are major employers as well. Ireland's Johnson Controls heads a modest list of area manufacturers. Importantly, Yuma is a border town, situated on the opposite side of a small Mexican town called San Luis Rio Colorado. About an hour's drive west is El Centro, California, and its Mexican neighbor Mexicali, a city with more than 1m people. The rise of northern Mexico's "maquiladora" factories following the NAFTA agreement in the 1990s led to more cross-border trade. The updated USMCA trade pact, coupled with the trend of multinational near-shoring, augurs well for additional trade growth. Still, Yuma is struggling. In a country where college education is a good predictor of higher income and positive social outcomes, Yuma doesn't even have a four-year institution of higher learning—it's the only major community in Arizona where that's the case. Only 15% of adults have a bachelor's degree, compared to nearly a third nationally. In August, Yuma had the second highest unemployment rate of any metro area tracked by the Labor Department—18%, besting only its neighbor El Centro (it was 14% even before the pandemic). Roughly two-thirds of the county's population identifies as Hispanic, more than half speaks a language other than English at home, and 26% are foreign born, which in most cases means across the border. Housing shortages are an issue, not least for military personnel relocating to the area. Health care professionals, in short supply, often have trouble finding adequate housing as well. Nearly 18% of residents don't have health insurance, compared to 10% nationally. The just-passed federal infrastructure bill should help with broadband access and managing the current western drought. Federal and state funds are also crucial to developing and maintaining worker training programs, business investment incentives and other measures to boost employment. Also important are tax incentives like foreign trade zones and opportunity zones. Federal Covid relief funding boosted local incomes during the pandemic. Now, the re-opening of the Canadian border provides a lift—As a New York Times report from earlier this month depicts, many Canadian "snowbirds" spend their winters in Yuma, at RV resorts and mobile home parks. While there, some cross the border for low-priced medical care, massages, manicures and entertainment. Less welcome are illegal immigrants attempting to cross the border near Yuma, putting the city on the front lines of a tense national political debate. Even less welcome is the Covid virus, which has hit the Yuma area hard.

(44)

HUNTSVILLE, ALABAMA

December 2021

Alabama, since becoming a state in 1819, hasn't exactly been a champion of Hamiltonian federal power. Yet federal dollars, deals and development are directly responsible for the prosperity of its second largest metro. Huntsville, in the north of the state near Tennessee's border, is in fact one of the *nation's* most dynamic economies, with a population that grew 13% during the 2010s—growth was just 3% in Birmingham, while Mobile and Montgomery *lost* people. Huntsville's unemployment rate today? Just 2%. The city's early economic life mirrored that of others in the deep South: Cotton trading, boosted later by railroads and textile mills, the latter fleeing higher labor costs in the North. As late as the Second World War, much of the South remained in extreme poverty. But the war was a major inflection point for the region's economic development, nowhere more so than in Huntsville. Then and there, the army established a facility for chemical munitions production and missile research. After the war, Germany's leading rocket and missile engineers were brought to Huntsville, helping the U.S. in its Cold War arms race with the Soviet Union. The city also played a leading role in the mission to land a man on the moon. Defense contractors from the private sector naturally followed. And today, the U.S. Army's Redstone Arsenal, along with NASA's co-located Marshall Space Flight Center, employ more than 44,000 people in Huntsville. So while other areas of the South focused on development tied to (most importantly) the auto sector, national defense and the space economy remain central in Huntsville—hence its nickname, the "Rocket City." The space economy, indeed, seems poised for future growth as companies like SpaceX develop new services. Blue Origin, owned by Amazon founder Jeff Bezos, opened a $200m rocket engine factory in Huntsville just last year. Around the same time, NASA awarded nearly $1b worth of contracts to SpaceX, Blue Origin and a Huntsville-based company called Dynetics, Inc. Their task: To build a lunar landing system in hopes of reinvigorating manned space flight. Companies like Boeing, Northrop Grumman and Lockheed all have major offices in the area. Another large employer is Virginia-based SAIC, also a top defense contractor. Many such firms are located at the Cummings Research Park, the second largest of its type after Raleigh-Durham's Research Triangle. Nearby is the University of Alabama's Huntsville campus, with about 10,000 students. The region's largest employer other than the army base is the local non-profit hospital system. But overall, government, including state and local government, accounts for almost a quarter of all nonfarm payroll jobs in the Huntsville metro. That includes the FBI, which considers Huntsville its second headquarters after Washington. The auto industry, to be clear, does play a meaningful role in Huntsville's economy, just not a dominant role as in say, Greenville-Spartanburg. Mazda and Toyota will soon jointly open a $2.3b plant in Huntsville, employing 4,000 people. Navistar International produces commercial trucks and busses there as well. As the metro grows, Amazon is responding with a second fulfilment center. Late next year, Discovery Life Sciences will open a new headquarters, boosting the city's biotech credentials. Nevertheless, it's defense and space that form the centerpiece of Huntsville's economy. And given the skillsets required for activities like rocket building, it's no wonder that 43% of adults in surrounding Madison County have college degrees, compared to 32% nationwide and 26% statewide. The metro area remains relatively small, ranking just 117th in the U.S. in 2019. It's moving up the rankings however, and punches far above its weight economically. Unlike the Rocket Man Elton John, this Rocket City need not wait a long, long time for takeoff.

(4 5)

UPPER PENINSULA, MICHIGAN

December 2021

There are no shuttered auto factories in this part of Michigan. Just shuttered mines, shuttered timber companies and a shuttered Air Force Base. Shattered, meanwhile, are dreams and goals of growing the local economy, something hard to do with a shrinking population. The large area of northern Michigan called the Upper Peninsula, territorially disconnected from the rest of the state, has all too many of the unfortunate hallmarks of struggling rural America. A declining and aging population stands among them, with too few jobs to retain natives, let alone attract newcomers. The U.P., surrounded by the Great Lakes, is home to about 300,000 people today, a 3% decline from ten years ago. In Luce County, one of 15 counties on the island, population plummeted by 20%. In some areas, some 40% of all residents are over 65, compared to 17% nationally. The U.P.'s struggles aren't new. The height of its prosperity was roughly 100 years ago, when its iron ore and copper helped fuel America's early industrialization. But much of the mineral wealth was eventually depleted—the last copper mine closed in 1995. Just one major iron ore mine remains, owned by Cliffs Natural resources and located not far from Marquette—that's the U.P.'s largest town with about 20,000 people. Not far is the country's only high-grade nickel mine, though deposits will run out by 2025. During its heyday, immigrants poured in to work the mines, from England, Ireland, Germany, Canada and—most unusually—Finland (roughly 35% of today's U.P. residents claim Finnish heritage). As mines disappeared, the K.I. Sawyer Air Force Base helped cushion the blow. But that closed in 1995. What's left is an economy highly dependent on the bedrock sectors of health care, local government and education. That includes Marquette General Hospital and Northern Michigan University. Cliffs, according to the Lake Superior Community Partnership, is the U.P.'s largest non-health care *private* employer (about a thousand jobs). Walmart ranks next. American Airlines operates a small maintenance base at Marquette's airport, where travelers can find nonstop flights to Chicago, Minneapolis and Detroit. Airports in Hancock, Sault Ste. Marie and a few other U.P. towns offer commercial air service, but only on small jets. Flights cater mostly to tourists, another critical component of the peninsula's economy. Visitors come mostly from mainland Michigan and neighboring states like Wisconsin. Some come from Canada, though the border was closed during much of the Covid crisis. Most come during summers, though winter sports are an attraction as well. So are casinos operated by Native American tribes. The U.P. is not an easy place for tourists to reach, however, with its limited air service and just one bridge link to the rest of Michigan. In a word, it's remote. For those living in the peninsula's west, Green Bay, Wisconsin, is the nearest population center. Like many rural communities across the U.S., attracting skilled workers was a challenge well before the pandemic. Now it's even tougher. Insufficient housing, a lack of childcare options, a dearth of broadband connections, limited ethnic and racial diversity and strained public budgets are all obstacles to recruiting teachers, engineers, public administrators, health care professionals and so on. Only 2% of the local population is foreign born. Agriculture isn't big simply because of the harsh weather. Real estate, on the other hand, is one area with some vibrancy, boosted by the market for short-term rentals to visitors. That can be controversial, given its impact on local housing costs. No less controversial are plans for a Canadian energy pipeline running through the U.P. The recently passed infrastructure bill, on top of three

Covid relief bills, have provided rural communities like the U.P. with a large quantity of available funds for development. Securing these new funds, sometimes through a grant process, presents a unique opportunity. But using the new money wisely is critical. One not-so-fun fact about Michigan: It was the only state in the U.S. to lose population between 2000 and 2010, before growing slightly (2%) during the 2010s. Detroit and its auto sector, of course, heavily influence Michigan's demographic destiny. But declines in the Upper Peninsula aren't helping.

JACKSON HEIGHTS, NEW YORK

January 2022

f immigrants make you uncomfortable, don't come here. In the shadows of Manhattan's skyscrapers, in the borough of Queens, lies a remarkable neighborhood where a stunning 60% of residents were born outside of the United States. Of these, 65% are Hispanic—Ecuadorians are the largest group, followed by Dominicans, Mexicans, Colombians and Peruvians. But if you visit, you'll hardly hear just Spanish. Another 9% of the neighborhood's 175,000 people hail from Bangladesh. Immigrants from China and India account for an additional 8%. All told, Jackson Heights residents are said to speak 167 different languages—a true mixing and mashup of the world's peoples if ever there was one. You won't just *hear* the neighborhood's international diversity though. You'll see it, most visibly in the area's shops and restaurants. Not uncommon are blocks with say, an Argentine restaurant next to a Russian sweet shop beside an Indian jeweler adjacent to a Peruvian nightclub connected to a Korean nail salon. It wasn't always this way. Jackson Heights was developed in the early 1900s as a *refuge* for native-born New Yorkers looking to flee the immigrant masses of Manhattan. One neighborhood history by Hunter College professor Ines

Miyares described it as "intended to be an exclusive suburban community for White, nonimmigrant Protestants within a close commute of Midtown Manhattan." The post-World War II rise of suburbia, however, saw this role of refuge move to New Jersey, Long Island and Westchester County. In the meantime, Jackson Heights endured the suburban exodus along with the rest of New York City, most painfully during the dark days of the 1970s. It was a time, remember, when New York was losing garment industry jobs, shipping jobs and manufacturing jobs. Thanks to finance, media, health care, tourism and education jobs, the city's fortunes would rebound sharply in the 1990s. Manhattan, thereafter becoming unaffordable for most immigrants, was nevertheless a short 20-minute subway ride from Jackson Heights. Newcomers poured in, but so did many young professionals lured by lower rents, falling crime (major felonies dropped by 45% between 2000 and 2018) and the area's cultural and culinary vibrancy. Jackson Heights today is home to a large LGBTQ community as well (it's in fact the site of the annual Queens Pride parade). LaGuardia airport is minutes away. So is Citi Field (where the New York Mets play baseball) and Arthur Ashe stadium (site of the U.S. Open tennis tournament). According to a report by the New York State Comptroller, payrolls and tax receipts grew faster in Jackson Heights than the city as a whole during much of the 2010s. By 2018, the unemployment rate was just 4%. The poverty rate fell from 20% in 2010 to 13% in 2017, significantly lower than the citywide rate and the second-largest decline among the city's 55 neighborhoods. From 2009 to 2018, Jackson Heights welcomed 660 new businesses, many of them small shops and restaurants operated by immigrants. The area has many doctor and dental offices too, along with diagnostic laboratories and home health care services. Outside of health care, some of the most common jobs among residents are construction workers, housekeepers, janitors, taxi drivers, retail workers, restaurant workers, administrative assistants and office clerks, all living alongside upper income professionals and knowledge sector workers. It's not an entirely happy story though. Jackson Heights is more affordable than Manhattan, for sure, but still expensive, increasingly so as more affluent people move in. The Comptroller report noted a 26% increase in median rents between 2009 and 2017, far outpacing a 10% increase in neighborhood incomes. Schools in the area are overcrowded. Nearly 30% of residents lack health insurance, more than twice the citywide figure. In 2017, 13% of households received Supplemental Nutrition Assistance Program benefits (or SNAP, also known as food stamps). More than 40% relied on Medicaid, the federal-state program for insuring the health of low-income Americans. In 2014, a quarter of homes reported the presence of cockroaches! Only 20% of adults hold a college degree. And less than half can speak English proficiently. New York's immigrant heavy neighborhoods also worry their populations were undercounted by the 2020 Census, which leads to under-representation in political bodies like the U.S. Congress. As it happens, Jackson Heights is represented in Congress by one of America's most famous politicians: Alexandria Ocasio-Cortez, or "AOC." She was the only Democrat in the House of Representatives, incidentally, that voted *against* the 2020 CARES Act providing relief from the Covid crisis, feeling it didn't provide enough relief to the "hardest hit Congressional district in the country." Jackson Heights was indeed hit hard. According to NYC Health (as of Dec. 23rd) nearly 400 residents have died of the virus. Many of the deaths occurred early in the pandemic, and vaccination rates today are extremely high. Naturally, the neighborhood's post-pandemic future will depend a lot on the fortunes of New York City's economic rebound. In the meantime, Jackson Heights continues to evolve economically. A new Target store just opened on one busy shopping street, amid evergreen tensions between protecting the neighborhood's small businesses from Big Box competition on the one hand and addressing the interests of area consumers on the other. The fact is, Target can charge lower prices and offer more selection. But does it destroy the middle-class shopkeeper and mess with the neighborhood's character?

CINCINNATI, OHIO

January 2022

For some cities, past is prologue. As early as the 1830s, Cincinnati was in the right place at the right time. The young city, built along the Ohio River, was perfectly situated for the newly-emerging age of river commerce—so much so that it became the first city in the Midwest to crack the top ten ranking of America's most populous cities. Many less-welcoming developments have occurred in the nearly two centuries since, from the rise of mightier midwestern cities like Chicago (after the Civil War) to the region's deindustrialization (after World War II). But Cincinnati, the "Queen City," suddenly finds itself once again in the right place at the right time, in this case for the age of e-commerce. Last summer, Amazon opened a $1.5b air cargo hub at Cincinnati's airport (located on the Kentucky side of the Ohio River). It now serves as the company's primary U.S. hub for air cargo, turning Cincinnati into North America's seventh busiest cargo airport. It's not just Amazon. Germany's DHL uses Cincinnati as its chief North American hub too. As local development officials like to stress, the city lies within 500 miles of nearly 60% of the U.S. population, underscoring its utility as a logistics hub. And not just for airlines. CSX, the railroad, operates one of the country's largest railyards in Cincinnati. Wayfair, the online retailer, operates a 900,000 square foot fulfillment center near the airport. It's Amazon, however, that most forcefully highlights the city's burgeoning leadership in moving goods. It no longer, incidentally, plays much of a role in moving people—not since Delta Air Lines closed its hub there. That was long before the Covid crisis, which even while turbocharging air cargo, rained havoc on passenger aviation. One of the chief victims: General Electric's Cincinnati-based aircraft engine division, a high-tech manufacturing giant. GE Engines isn't the city's largest employer, however. That distinction belongs to Kroger, the country's largest supermarket chain. The world-renown Cincinnati Children's Hospital is the area's second largest employer. The University of Cincinnati is important as well. So is Fifth-Third, one of the country's largest banks. But Cincinnati's most famous company? Surely that's Procter & Gamble, whose products—Tide, Bounty, Pampers, Crest, Charmin, Gillette, Old Spice—are in every American's home. This is not, to be clear, the story of an American superstar city. Like much of the Midwest, Cincinnati continues to lose people to the Sun Belt. It hasn't produced a high-tech economy comparable to nearby Pittsburgh. And it's still much smaller than Chicago or Detroit. The metro area grew merely 4% during the 2010s, leaving it the 30th largest in the country. Nor is Cincinnati's urban core a big selling point for luring young brains. The city's population peaked in 1950. And while residents did start trickling back in the 2010s thanks to new development and new attractions, recent comments by a local sports star captured the city's underwhelming image: "Fortunately, there's not a ton to do in Cincinnati, so nobody's going out to clubs and bars and getting Covid every weekend," said Cincinnati Bengals quarterback Joe Burrow last month. Newly elected mayor Aftab Pureval acknowledges the brand problem, which he notes is ironic in a city that's home to one of the world's leaders in brand marketing—maybe P&G can help with that. Pureval's other priorities include affordable housing, crime, climate resilience and racial equality. Last year, incidentally, marked the 20th anniversary of major racial unrest in the city. City Council corruption scandals are another blight. Pureval, in an interview on local TV station WLWT, also highlighted the risk to city tax revenues from people working remotely rather than in downtown offices. Washington's infrastructure bill, on the other hand, will deliver new revenues for projects like the upgrading of key bridges crossing the Ohio. True, the Ohio isn't the commercial superhighway it was in the age of river commerce. Long gone are the days when Irish and German immigrants arrived in great numbers to staff meatpacking plants and iron foundries. But also gone are the days when the city was losing population, and when the area economy struggled to modernize. Today, Cincinnati has its solid base of corporate giants, led by P&G, GE and Kroger. It has its large health care sector. And it's once again central to the arteries of commerce, not as a river port but as an airline hub for moving freight. Those packages that just showed up at your door? They might very well have journeyed through Cincinnati.

GREAT FALLS, MONTANA

January 2022

Just look at a map. Montana is a big, big state. Only Alaska, California and Texas have more land. But not too many people live in Montana—about as many (1.1m) as live in Rhode Island. That said, only one state (Idaho) grew its population faster last year. Indeed, people are moving to Montana. But only to certain parts of the state. They're coming in droves to Bozeman, home to a large university, stunning scenery and soaring home prices. They're coming to Missoula, another scenic university town. They're coming to Billings, with its large energy sector. They're coming (with lots of money) to Kalispell, gateway to Glacier National Park. They're coming to Helena, the state capital. But people are *not*—at least not yet—coming to places farther east and north of the Rockies, including Great Falls, still the state's third largest population center after Billings and Missoula. The Great Falls metro area, alas, had fewer residents in 2019 than it had in 2010. And its real GDP grew a mere 7% from 2007 (the year before the Great Recession) to 2018. The local economy shrank, unsurprisingly, in 2020, due to the pandemic. But it shrank in 2019 as well. As the Montana Historical Society explains, most of the state's towns and cities came into existence—typically in the latter half of the 1800s—for three main reasons: agriculture, transportation and mining. Sure enough, the area around Great Falls contains farmland raising products like wheat and barley. The railroad came through in the 1880s. And with respect to mining, Great Falls benefitted indirectly. The town of Butte, once bustling with copper mines, needed a place to send the copper, to turn it into wiring. Great Falls proved the ideal place, thanks to its abundance of cheap hydroelectric energy. With dam construction, the Missouri River waterfalls provided the power to build a thriving industrial economy, one that would make Great Falls the largest city in the state until the 1990s. The city got another boost during World War II, when the military selected it to host an Air Force base. Malmstrom base remains central to the Great Falls economy today—it's the area's largest employer. But the military base, like the city's industrial base, has gotten smaller in recent decades, largely explaining the downward population trend. This is not, however, a story of rural despair. A closer look shows Great Falls reasonably well-positioned to grow again. For starters, it sits in the foothills of a Rocky Mountain region that's performed perhaps better than anywhere else during the pandemic. As other parts of Montana see home prices skyrocket, Great Falls remains affordable. The unemployment rate is just 2.4%, below where it was pre-Covid. Foreign manufacturers from Canada to Japan are enticed by the area's highway links along the Calgary-to-Salt Lake City corridor, all the way down to Mexico. No less attractive are BNSF railway links to the booming Pacific Northwest and its export-oriented seaports. Great Falls is also attracting business support services including call centers, aided by its lowish labor costs, neutral English accents and convenient time zone. Agribusiness and health care are other growing sectors. A new medical school will open next year. And a research center focused on Alzheimer's disease is expanding. Cargill and Centene are two national giants with a significant presence in Great Falls. Naturally, competing with Yellowstone and Glacier National Parks makes standing out as a tourist draw challenging. But the nearby mountains, outdoor sports and Native American culture lure a fair share of visitors, and potentially more remote workers as well. Make no mistake: The decline of copper mining in Butte many decades ago dealt a great blow to Great Falls. And it doesn't quite have the mountain-life appeal that's turning places like Bozeman into 21st century all-star economies. Nor does it have a large university. Nor is it the seat of state government. But it might just have enough to start growing again.

HARTFORD, CONNECTICUT

January 2022

I t's one of the smallest states in the country. But Connecticut is also one of the wealthiest per capita. It helps that towns like Stamford and Greenwich are within commuting distance to New York City. These places are home to the largest agglomeration of hedge funds outside of New York, led by Ray Dalio's Bridgewater Associates (AQR Capital, Viking Global and Tudor Investments are some others). The average wage for financial service workers in the area, according to the Stamford Advocate, is a princely $266,000. Moving eastward along the state's coast toward Boston, you'll find New Haven, home to Yale University. Still farther down the coast is New London, where General Dynamics builds multi-billion-dollar submarines for the U.S. Navy. Also along the coast are Native American casinos. Connecticut's largest city Hartford though, isn't on the coast. It's located in the center of the state. And its economic picture is more complicated, not exactly reflective of Connecticut's image as a prosperous land of money managers, Ivy League professors and Naval leaders. Hartford was, to be sure, once upon a time among America's wealthiest cities. But that was during the late 19th century, when it evolved into ground zero for the insurance industry. That distinction still holds true today, topping even Des Moines, Iowa, in insurance company heft. Hartford-based companies include health insurers like Cigna and Aetna (the latter now owned by CVS) and property/casualty insurers like The Hartford, a company founded in 1810. Insurers with corporate headquarters elsewhere, like New York City-based Travelers, typically have large office footprints in Hartford. Together with manufacturing and state government (Hartford is Connecticut's capital), insurance helped make central Connecticut an economic powerhouse through the first half of the 20th century. It doesn't quite hold that status today, however. The fact is, jobs in all three sectors—insurance, manufacturing and government— have contracted since the start of the millennium, according to a 2019 HUD report. A 2003 New York Times article entitled "Hartford Is No Longer the Insurance Capital" proved hyperbolic. In fact, it still is top dog for insurance. But due to mergers, divestitures and layoffs, the area's financial sector (including insurance) saw employment drop from 70,000 in 2000 to 57,200 in 2019. Between 2007 and 2019, the overall metro economy grew a mere 5%. Population, meanwhile, shrank 1% during the 2010s. Connecticut, once a hotspot for companies fleeing urban centers like New York, more recently has a history of seeing companies flee for greener pastures. These include giants like UPS, which left for Atlanta in 1994, and GE, which left for Boston in 2016. Hartford itself lost many headquarters over the years, not to mention its only major league sports franchise—NHL's Whalers left for North Carolina in 1997. More recently, the merger between Raytheon and Connecticut's United Technologies saw HQ jobs move to the Boston area. The state, by the way, didn't have a personal income tax until the early 1990s. The Hartford region also lost jobs in gun manufacturing, something it was known for in the early days of the industrial revolution. Connecticut's capital, alas, has a legacy of problems familiar to most northeastern cities, including de-industrialization, suburbanization and discriminatory practices that left large racial gaps in wealth, income, home ownership and access to good schools. Unflatteringly, Hartford today looks more like Baltimore than Boston, in other words, a city with no shortage of wealthy suburbs but a deeply troubled inner core. The city of Hartford, according to Census data, has a poverty rate of nearly 30%, with more than a quarter of adults over 25 lacking even a high school degree. Among residents, 38% identify as Black; 44% also or separately identify as Hispanic. Hartford is also a much smaller city than even Baltimore—the metro area ranks number 49 by population nationwide (Baltimore is 21). So it doesn't have the tourism economy that even Baltimore has, let alone what New York and Boston have. A better comparison might be to Trenton, another northeastern state capital with strikingly similar demographic data (the poverty rate for one is almost identical). Hartford, furthermore, lacks the downtown amenities and housing that help attract knowledge workers—many prefer to live in places like New York and Boston. To be clear, Hartford has made progress in this area, investing in urban renewal projects. It's also, like so many areas across America, getting a boost from the booming transportation and distribution sector. Sure enough, Amazon has a major presence in Hartford, conveniently located roughly halfway between Boston and New York, not to mention within an eight-hour drive of 30m Canadians. State and local government jobs help anchor the labor market, as do health care jobs. The local power provider Eversource is a big metro area employer. So is the University of Connecticut. Also notable is the sports channel ESPN, recent layoffs there notwithstanding. The region, long a magnet for migrants from Puerto Rico, continues to attract people from the island. Clearly, the dawning age of remote working is an opportunity, with all those hedge fund, university and defense contracting jobs within comfortable reach if only commuting there two or three days per week. Same for jobs in Providence, New York and Boston (though inconveniently, Hartford is *not* on Amtrak's busy northeast corridor line). As MetroHartford Alliance likes to say, citing a 2019 C2ER study, living costs in Connecticut's capital are 21% cheaper than in Boston, and 34% cheaper than in New York. Perhaps a good place to move after all… especially if you're in the insurance business.

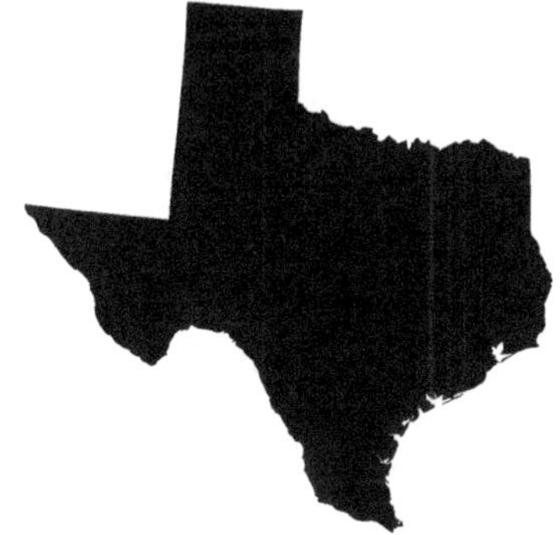

MIDLAND, TEXAS

January 2022

Quiz: What was the fastest-growing metro area in Texas during the 2010s? A) Houston, B) Austin or C) Dallas-Fort Worth. The answer is D) none of the above. In a state blanketed by scorching-hot economies, none saw its population grow faster than the Midland-Odessa metro in dusty West Texas. The reason is simple: oil and gas. According to the U.S. Energy Information Administration, the Texas Midland Basin (part of the giant Permian basin) generated 1.68m barrels of crude oil per day in 2020, or a fifth of all crude oil production in the U.S. It also produced about 6% of America's dry natural gas. Midland and Odessa, separated by a short drive, are quintessential U.S. oil towns, originally founded as sleepy railway stops for cattle traders. But the area became a critical node in global energy markets ever since the first West Texas oil strikes in the 1920s. In fact, oil prices today are typically quoted using the WTI benchmark, which stands for West Texas Intermediate. It's here in the dry isolated plains between Dallas-Fort Worth and El Paso that a young George H.W. Bush and his son began their journeys to the White House. It's here where non-college educated workers routinely earn six-figure salaries. It's here where nearly a third of all jobs are in natural resource mining or construction. It's here in the 2010s, furthermore, where America's shale oil fracking revolution took center stage, reinvigorating the U.S. energy sector and greatly mitigating the country's dependence on foreign oil. Population growth between 2010 and 2019 was an astounding 29%, fourth highest among all U.S. metros behind only The Villages, Myrtle Beach and Austin. People didn't come for the pretty scenery. They came to make money, as many did. While much of the U.S. economy endured a painfully slow recovery from the 2008-09 recession, Midland's real GDP tripled from 2007 to 2019. Odessa is considerably poorer but in Midland, where much of the area's wealth is concentrated, real annual per capita income in 2020 was $108,000, making it one of America's richest cities. The simple fact is, oil is the world's most important commodity, and the Permian Basin has one of the world's most prolific reserves. The oil market, however, notoriously booms and busts, taking Midland-Odessa along for the ups and downs. During the 1950s and 1960s, Ivy League-educated northeasterners like George Bush Sr. came to town seeking fortunes. The 1970s were a golden age. But the oil bust of the 1980s and '90s hit Midland hard. By the 2000s, it seemed, oil supplies were running out. That is until new horizontal drilling technologies captured previously inaccessible supplies, ushering in another mega-boom between 2010 and 2015. Lo and behold, then came another crash. In 2016, an article from the Texas Tribune described the situation like this: "Thousands have been laid off. Tax collections are plummeting. Many are on the brink of homelessness. Rows of drilling rigs and white company trucks sit idle—there's no telling for how long." Real median household income in Midland-Odessa, according to the Dallas Fed, fell 13% from 2014 to 2016. The pandemic brought another roller-coaster ride, with oil prices plummeting early on and then rebounding sharply. The area's largest energy sector employers like Pioneer, Salisbury, Keene, Endeavor and Haliburton are all breathing a sigh of relief. Development officials are attempting to diversify the economy, opening a new engineering school in 2017. Wind farms are prevalent in the area, which is also home to a space port. Downtown development projects seek to lure families and young professionals. The Dallas Fed does note that oil production is becoming less labor intensive with new technologies, implying fewer opportunities for less educated workers even during boom times. Roughly half of Midland-Odessa's people, by the way, are of Hispanic origin. In general, though, the population is highly transient, with many coming just to work for a few years before moving elsewhere. A housing shortage during boom times is a challenge. So is periodic drought. Much more unnerving for Midland-Odessa, however, is the prospect of a world that powers its vehicles and heats its homes without the need for hydrocarbons.

MAUI, HAWAII

February 2022

Golden beaches, bright blue waters and lush green hills. Everyday sunshine too. Are there any places on earth more inviting than the island of Maui? To visitors, maybe not. To those in search of economic opportunity, however, Maui is a distant way from paradise. It was only in 1959 that Hawaii became a U.S. state, with its capital in Honolulu, a metro area that today has nearly 1m residents. There, national defense plays an outsized role in the economy, perhaps more so than even tourism. According to the state's Department of Business, Economic Development and Tourism (DBEDT), Washington's $7.7b worth of annual defense spending in Hawaii accounts for nearly 9% of the state's GDP. Honolulu alone has nine military installations, the largest and most famous being Joint Base Pearl Harbor. Including civilian personnel, these installations employ roughly 65,000 people. But little of this spending touches Maui, Hawaii's third most populous island with about 120,000 residents, most living in and around the main town of Kahului. In the 19th century, people came to Maui from as far away as New England, engaged in whaling, logging or trade with Asia. Some came as religious missionaries. Sugar, pineapple and cattle became the island's chief agricultural products. Today, however, production of pretty much anything in Maui is cost prohibitive—high labor costs, high transport costs, high energy costs and high property costs. Almost everything needs to thus be imported. The final sugar cane operation closed in 2016. The island no longer produces meaningful quantities of commercial milk or dairy products. The Maui Land and Pineapple company? It no longer grows pineapples. Lahaina, Maui, furthermore, once served as Hawaii's capital before Honolulu assumed that role in the 1840s. Contemporary Maui does have *some* defense related activity, including an Air Force research lab. The island is playing a modest role in the emerging space economy too, thanks in part to the University of Hawaii's Institute for Astronomy. Boeing does some work on the island as well. Naturally, health care and education account for a sizeable chunk of jobs. The Maui Memorial Medical Center is in fact the island's largest employer. Most other major employers are hotels, led by the Grand Wailea Resort. Maui is thus a poster child for tourism-dependent economies, which meant big trouble when the pandemic hit in March 2020. In May of that year, Maui County's unemployment rate hit a shocking 33%. As late as June 2021, it was still in double digits. Today it's down to 6%, still roughly two points above the national average. Just 800,000 tourists came to Maui in 2020, down 74% from 2019. More than 2m came in 2021, but this was still far shy of the 3m-plus that came pre-Covid. December arrivals were still 15% below pre-Covid levels. An important distinction though: Hawaii's tourist sector from the rest of the U.S. is busier now than ever. What hasn't recovered is international tourism, most importantly from Japan. Inter-island cruise departures are just getting restarted. But domestic airline seats from Kahului airport this quarter are up 23% from Q1 2019, according to aviation data provider Cirium. Hawaiian Airlines, based in Honolulu, is Maui's largest airline. But growing aggressively is Southwest Airlines, which first entered the market in early 2019. One great tailwind to tourism demand was the long west coast U.S. tech boom centered in places like the San Francisco Bay Area, Los Angeles and Seattle. Thanks to the rise of companies like Apple, Google and Amazon, west coast disposable income for vacations grew enormously during the 2010s and—fortunately for Maui—never stopped growing throughout the pandemic. This bodes well for domestic demand in 2022 and beyond, complemented at some point by a return of Japanese, Canadian and other foreign visitors… assuming, that is, they're welcome. Last month, Maui's City Council voted to approve a controversial moratorium on new hotels and visitor lodgings. Why? Because of an outcry among locals about rising home prices, environmental degradation and snarled traffic. Affordable housing is a major problem in Maui, which also has the effect of deterring remote workers. A University of Hawaii study gave a familiar explanation of why it's so difficult to build new housing, an explanation applicable to many areas of the U.S. It wrote:

> *"Neighborhood residents often oppose affordable housing due to likely increases in traffic congestion and public school crowding as well as concerns about the impact of denser low-income housing on housing values, view lines and neighborhood aesthetics. Opposition often takes the form of residents petitioning in neighborhood board or county council committee hearings for costly changes in the project's density, parking capacity, building heights and setbacks and supporting infrastructure. The process of negotiating and obtaining approvals for changes in plans raises project costs and reduces projected project revenues by pushing out the time to project approval and completion. In many cases project developers abandon projects or never propose them in the first place because of the higher development costs and longer project timeline that the current approval process entails."*

To escape the high cost of living, many in Maui have migrated to mainland cities like Las Vegas for work—the island's population did grow a solid 8% during the 2010s however, thanks to growing leisure and hospitality employment. Development officials hope to attract more non-tourist businesses with pitches like: "Hawaii is the only state in the U.S. where a phone call to New York and a phone call to Tokyo can occur in the typical business day." The new infrastructure bill will provide funds to upgrade Maui's harbor facilities. Oracle billionaire Larry Ellison is a notable investor in the area. Film production is another potential growth area. Nothing, however, can replace tourism.

LEHIGH VALLEY, PENNSYLVANIA

February 2022

Billy Joel understood. "They're closing all the factories down… and it's getting very hard to stay." So sang the singer in "Allentown," his 1982 portrait of American deindustrialization. By the mid-1990s, even the mighty Bethlehem Steel was largely gone, leaving northeastern Pennsylvania limping into the new millennia with bleak economic prospects. Sure enough, many of America's old industrial regions never did regain their footing, some still looking for answers in the 2020s. Not the Lehigh Valley though. If Billy Joel were to write a song about Allentown today, it would tell of warehouses and health care facilities *opening up*, making it hard for many jobseekers *not* to come. Allentown and its neighboring cities of Bethlehem and Easton aren't exactly replicating the spectacular booms of Sun Belt superstar metros like Austin, Orlando or Nashville. The Valley's combined metro area saw population grow just 3% during the 2010s (Austin grew 29%). But don't let that mask what's been a remarkable economic renaissance, one less heralded but no less impressive than Pittsburgh's revival in Pennsylvania's west. Unlike Pittsburgh, the Lehigh Valley isn't on anyone's list of 21st century information technology hubs. It has nothing quite comparable to Pittsburgh's leadership in artificial intelligence and autonomous driving. Yet the Valley—Pennsylvania's third largest metro after Philadelphia and Pittsburgh—punches above its weight in advanced health care and life sciences. The health care sector is the area's largest employer. Manufacturing is still very much alive in the Valley, accounting for 16% of economic production, compared to 13% nationally. It's not making steel anymore. It's instead making transportation equipment (Mack Trucks has a factory near Allentown), pharmaceuticals, medical devices, industrial products and even crayons—Crayola is headquartered in Easton. These days, supporting a manufacturing economy isn't about supplying cheap labor, but rather skilled labor. That underscores the importance of the Valley's colleges, most importantly Lehigh University, renowned for its engineering program (the late auto exec Lee Iacocca is a famous alum). The school is also one of the region's top employers. But can education, health care and modern manufacturing really bury the ghosts of steel? According to the Department of Housing and Urban Development, Bethlehem Steel alone employed 300,000 people nationwide during World War II. The manufacturing sector, in fact, continued to decline well into the new millennia, shedding more than 2,000 jobs between 2001 and 2007. By then, however, a new engine of economic growth was taking shape across America, one exemplified by California's Inland Empire. There, a hub had emerged for storing, sorting and distributing the tsunami of goods entering the ports of Los Angeles and Long Beach. Land and labor are much cheaper there than in and around pricey L.A. Yet it's close enough, not just to handle L.A.'s imports but all the e-commerce deliveries bound for America's second largest consumer market. But what about America's *largest* consumer market? What location had low enough costs, sufficient highway access and ample enough land to conveniently distribute goods into and out of the New York City metro, not to mention nearby Philadelphia? The Lehigh Valley fits the bill, thus transforming into an east coast Inland Empire. From 2000 to 2018, the area's jobs in transportation and utilities more than doubled from 12,000 to nearly 30,000. And that was before the pandemic-era surge in e-commerce. This past holiday season, Amazon alone recruited 800 additional seasonal workers at its multiple Leigh Valley facilities. FedEx has one of its largest ground facilities worldwide near Allentown. Job offers are everywhere, screaming from billboard after billboard along highways running into and out of the city. Route 78 runs straight to New York, just 90 miles to the east. Others run straight into Philadelphia, 60 miles to the south. Warehouse construction sites are everywhere. So are trucks moving along the highways—not always to the liking of local residents. Last May, the New York Times profiled the Valley's e-commerce boom, noting that "manufacturing jobs in the Lehigh Valley pay, on average, $71,400 a year, compared with $46,700 working in a warehouse or driving a truck." Still, that's attractive in a country where good jobs for non-college graduates are increasingly scarce. They're jobs, furthermore, where pay has risen sharply during the pandemic, and which can't be outsourced to Mexico or China—though robots and autonomous trucks are a threat. Like pretty much everywhere else across America, it's not easy finding enough warehouse workers and truck drivers in the Valley right now. Affordable housing is another local malady, mirroring national trends. According to the Greater Lehigh Valley Realtors, home prices spiked 18% last year. Billy Joel would never have imagined *that* in the 1980s. He wouldn't have imagined that in the early 2000s. The Valley has even become a magnet of sorts for immigrants, especially Latin American and Caribbean families priced out of New York City and New Jersey (in 2016, 12% of the Valley's population identified as Puerto Rican). Casino gambling has drawn nearby tourists—Sands Bethworks Gaming is the metro area's third largest non-government employer. Downtown revitalization has drawn newcomers. And the Lehigh Valley Economic Development Corporation (LVEDC) highlights the Covid-era emergence of "super commuters" with hybrid jobs in cities like New York and Philadelphia. Amtrak, incidentally, is pushing for a direct rail link to New York. Allegiant, meanwhile, America's most profitable airline, is expanding air service to Florida from Lehigh Valley's main airport. Time to write a new song, Billy.

BENTONVILLE, ARKANSAS

February 2022

One hundred years after the Civil War, in the 1960s, nearly half of all Arkansas residents were still living below the poverty line, more than double the national average. Today, the figure is closer to 15%, which still makes it the fifth poorest state by this measure, but only three points above the national average. Arkansas, so it happens, touches two of the most impoverished regions of the country: The Mississippi Delta in the southeast and the Ozark Mountains in the northwest. In between, meanwhile, are distressed economies like Pine Bluff—Pine Bluff was the fastest shrinking metro in the entire United States last decade. The Delta region, too, remains troubled, with poverty rates still roughly double the national average. The Ozarks, however, tell a much happier story. The state's three main Ozark counties—Benton, Madison and Washington—have gone from having poverty rates roughly double the national average in 1960 to roughly equal to the national average today, according to the St. Louis Fed. A big reason is the University of Arkansas, located in the area's largest city Fayetteville. Close to 30,000 students attend the school, a public institution. The greatest gains in wealth though, have occurred north of Fayetteville, in and near Benton County. There, three corporate giants loom large, giving the county itself a poverty rate that's now *lower* than the national average. One of these giants is Tyson Foods, a poultry processor and retailer. Another is the trucking and logistics firm J.B. Hunt, also a Fortune 500 company. But neither come close in influence to Walmart, the single largest corporation in the country by sales—it's the country's largest private-sector employer as well. Northwest Arkansas wouldn't be anyone's first guess as the home of America's largest company. But so it is. And so the retailer has delivered nothing short of an economic miracle to a once destitute region. Walmart, founded in Benton County 60 years ago by entrepreneur Sam Walton, has a global workforce exceeding 2m people today, 28,000 of them in the Fayetteville-Bentonville metro area. That doesn't include another 10,000 or so employed by various Walmart suppliers with offices in the area. HUD Department figures show that Walmart, Tyson and the University of Arkansas alone account for 16% of all jobs in the area—a metro area that grew in population by 21% during the 2010s. Very few places in the country grew that fast. In fact, only 14 other metros did—most of them more familiar growth stories—Austin, Raleigh-Durham, Orlando, Boise and Midland-Odessa, for example. Remember, Pine Bluff, just a four-hour drive from Bentonville, was the fastest-*shrinking* metro last decade, in part because people fled to Ozark region for jobs. A company the size of Walmart can indeed move mountains, even in the once-impoverished Ozark mountains. Last summer, the New York Times featured a story about Northwest Arkansas, highlighting its demographic changes. As recently as 1990, it was 95% White. Today the figure is more like 72% following an influx of immigrants taking jobs from processing chicken for Tyson to managing IT for Walmart. Springdale, home to Tyson, is now 38% Hispanic. Bentonville has a new Hindu temple. Labor Department data, by the way, showed a 16% y/y increase in average weekly wages in Benton County during the second quarter of 2019, *before* the pandemic put upward pressure on pay. No other large county in the country saw higher wage gains. But the pandemic exposed a major challenge. At a time of severe nationwide labor shortages, the extreme shortages of truck drivers and food processors are bedeviling Tyson and J.B. Hunt. It's at companies like these where sharp declines in immigration hurt most. That said, all three of Benton County's corporate giants are thriving financially, with Walmart announcing a $6b Q4 operating profit last week. The region, where housing prices are still relatively low, is attracting retirees as well. Walmart, meanwhile, is building a new headquarter campus, creating construction jobs. Things have come a long way since the federal housing department published an economic study of Northwest Arkansas in 1971. Poultry and the University were the twin pillars of the economy then. There was no mention of Walmart.

CHICAGO, ILLINOIS

February 2022

It's windy. Its shoulders are big. Its baseball teams are notoriously bad. We're talking, of course, about Chicago, America's third largest metro area behind New York and Los Angeles. It didn't even exist as a town until the 1830s, some 50 years after the U.S. won its independence from Britain. By early 19th century, however, it was already recognized for its strategic location along Lake Michigan. Farmers would travel to Chicago, where their products could move cheaply via the Great Lakes, the Erie Canal and the Atlantic Ocean, reaching their two largest markets of the time: the U.S. northeast and Europe. Before the days of the railroad, shipping by water was much faster and cheaper than shipping by land. But the railroads would soon come, making the Erie Canal obsolete. Not Chicago though. Far from losing its relevance, the city became the epicenter of the nation's railway system, a status it retains even today. Economically, no city benefitted more from the Civil War than Chicago. It was by then (the early 1860s) the dominant seller of grain, meat and lumber, all bought in mass quantities by the U.S. Army. According to William Cronon in his book "Nature's Metropolis," half of Chicago's 110,000 people in 1860 were immigrants, mostly from Ireland, Germany and Scandinavia. That helped make it America's eighth largest city at the time, up from 17th in the 1850 Census. Chicago continued to boom during the flourishing of America's post-Civil War industrial age, becoming a manufacturing powerhouse. From 1900 to 1950, it stood behind only New York in population, earning it the nickname "America's Second City." Railroads had lost some of their relevance in the age of airplanes and automobiles. But Chicago would become a premier center for aviation and trucking too. It also gave birth to the great retail empires of the consumer age, most famously Sears but also Marshall Field and Montgomery Ward. It simultaneously retained its manufacturing clout, producing farm equipment, food, railroad cars, steel and lots more. Immigrants continued to come, from Poland, Italy, Russia and so on. Importantly, the Great Migration north brought large numbers of African Americans to Chicago, often filling factory jobs, including critical wartime production roles during both World Wars. The city's industrial shine, unfortunately, started wearing off in the second half of the 1900s. As the U.S. suburbanized and de-industrialized, the city of Chicago—like many large cities at the time—experienced urban decay, an outflow of affluent Whites, racial tensions, crime, municipal corruption, failing public schools and substandard housing. Robert Spinney's book "City of Big Shoulders" recounts the time in 1955 when Soviet officials visited Chicago's Henry Horner housing project, remarking afterward: "We would be thrown off our jobs in Moscow if we left unfinished walls like this." Washington didn't disagree, issuing a 1968 federal report that described Chicago's public housing projects as "remindful of gigantic filing cabinets with separate cubicles for each human household." Many surrounding suburbs, to be sure, thrived in the decades leading up to the new millennium. It's where many of Chicagoland's most iconic companies were headquartered, including McDonalds (Oak Brook) and United Airlines (Elk Grove). The downtown Loop, meanwhile, did retain a core of influential companies like Sears, housed in what was once the world's tallest building. The city, furthermore, during the first Mayor Daley administration, didn't experience quite the fiscal collapse that New York suffered in the 1970s. Nevertheless, as Spinney writes, the city lost 60% of its manufacturing jobs—60%!—between 1960 and 1995. Between 1973 and 1977 alone, total job losses amounted to 123,000. Another 83,000 disappeared in the early 1990s, a dark period for U.S. cities that coincided with surging crime rates. In the new millennium, would Chicago follow the troubled path of its neighboring industrial colossus Detroit, unable to recover from all those lost manufacturing jobs? Or would it follow the inspirational path of New York City, which successfully transitioned to a knowledge-based economy? Happily, Chicago would indeed join New York as an all-star global city, powered by a diverse set of industries. Chicago remains vital to airlines, railroads and trucking firms. It also remains home to many food producers. Tourism, including international arrivals and business conventions, has been a major driver of Chicago's renaissance. Like everywhere else in the 2000s, Chicago added jobs in health care and education. The University of Chicago has perhaps the most famous economics department of any school worldwide. Governments—federal, state, county and local—are top employers. The city is also home to some of the world's top consulting, accounting and legal firms, enticed by all the nonstop worldwide air service available from O'Hare airport—for one thing, you can get out and back to New York, Texas or California in a day. According to HUD, the population of Chicago's Loop doubled in the first 15 years of the 2000s. Boeing moved its headquarters from Seattle. United replaced Sears in what's now called the Willis Tower. McDonald's came to downtown as well. JPMorgan established a big Chicago presence when it merged with Jamie Dimon's Bank One in 2004. The next year, the White Sox baseball team actually won a World Series—their first in almost 90 years! Even more improbably, the Cubs won eleven years later, for the first time since the Roosevelt Administration—TEDDY Roosevelt! Chicago further gained worldwide notoriety when longtime resident Barack Obama became president in 2008. It's hard to think of any humans more globally famous than the Obamas, except perhaps Michael Jordan and Oprah Winfrey, two other Chicago figures. Michael Jackson, incidentally, is from Gary, Indiana, close enough to be a Chicago suburb. Bill Murray, Pearl Jam's Eddie Vedder… should we mention Kanye West? Ronald Reagan, by the way, is still the only president that was born in Illinois, though Hillary Clinton came close to become the second. (Reagan was born about two hours west of Chicago;

Abraham Lincoln, born in Kentucky, lived in the capital Springfield three hours southwest). Chicago naturally grappled with familiar big city problems even during the boom of the past twenty years. The question now is how much permanent damage the pandemic will do. In the half-decade leading up to 2020, Chicago was creating nearly 11,000 jobs a year in leisure and hospitality, many catering to visitors from abroad. They all disappeared when Covid arrived, and it's unclear how many will ultimately return. The city is seeing rising levels of crime again, and the work-from-home phenomenon is depressing downtown activity and transit usage. Chicagoland as a whole, meanwhile, was *alone* among America's top 20 metros to have *lost* population in the 2010s. Even its old rival St. Louis grew by half a percentage point. The Cubs, we should add, are back to being bad—they lost 91 games last year. The city itself grew a bit, however, thanks again to immigration, this time primarily from Latin America and Asia. According to the Chicago Sun-Times, Latinos now account for roughly 30% of the city's population, surpassing the Black population. Blacks have in fact been leaving the city in large numbers, many moving to booming Sun Belt metros like Dallas and Houston. Economic development officials, meanwhile, are touting Chicago's progressive social values. One thing Chicago doesn't have: Good weather. That didn't matter when it was the best place in America for farmers to move produce, or the best place through which to run a railroad. It's still the best place to do many things, including, apparently, running giant companies like United Airlines, McDonald's, Walgreens, Archer Daniels Midland, Allstate, Caterpillar and Abbot Labs. All feel Chicago is a good place to attract talent. But for growing a population, especially in a time of dwindling immigration, being a cold and windy city doesn't help. All else equal, most people want sunshine and warmth.

TRI-CITIES, WASHINGTON

March 2022

With apologies to Austin, Seattle might just be America's strongest economy right now. You know the reasons why: Amazon, Microsoft, Boeing, Costco, Starbucks… But hours east of the Cascade Mountains, in Washington State's south central region, there's a lesser-known economic boom taking shape. And it looks nothing like Seattle's boom. Kennewick, Richland and Pasco together constitute Washington's Tri-Cities metro area, modest in size with roughly 300,000 people. That's enough to make it the state's third largest metro after Seattle and Spokane (counting Vancouver, Washington, as part of the Portland, Oregon metro). More interestingly, Tri-Cities is Washington State's fastest-growing area, even exceeding Seattle's electrifying growth. It was in fact the nation's 30th fastest-growing metro nationwide during the 2010s, out of some 400 tracked by the U.S. Census. Population increased 17% over the decade, lured by sunny weather, outdoor activities, relatively affordable housing and nuclear waste. Wait, what? Nuclear waste? That story begins with the Great Depression of the 1930s, when New Deal engineering projects—the Hoover Dam is the most famous—created new population centers across previously uninhabited regions of the American west. As Pomona College historian Char Miller explains in a discussion with the publication "Governing," Denver, Phoenix, Tucson, Albuquerque, El Paso, Las Vegas, Phoenix, San Diego and even mighty Los Angeles all owe their existence to large federal infrastructure projects. The same is true for Tri-Cities, which depends on water and cheap power from the New Deal-era Grand Coulee Dam to its north. Even today, such projects provide Washington State with some of the country's cheapest electric power. During the 1940s though, cheap and abundant power was prized for another reason: The development of atomic weapons. Tri-Cities was selected as a major research site for the Manhattan Project, America's secret plan to develop a nuclear bomb. The Hanford nuclear plant, more specifically, produced the required plutonium, along with electricity, from 1943 until its closure in 1987. Together with its research arm (which became the Pacific Northwest National Laboratory in the 1960s), the federal Hanford plant dominated the local Tri-Cities economy. By the mid-1980s, a quarter of its workforce, and a fifth its salaries and wages, were tied to federal dollars. When the plant closed in 1987, however, the federal money didn't disappear. Instead, Hanford became a giant cleanup site, one of 15 such Department of Energy (DOE) projects nationwide. For years, solid and liquid waste was buried underground, contaminating ground water and soils. The DOE and six major contractors currently have some 10,000 people working on the cleanup, which is expected to continue into at least the 2060s. Soon, a new $17b plant will turn some of the liquid waste into glass through a process called vitrification. In the meantime, the Pacific Northwest National Laboratory (PNNL) has become a federally-funded economic force in its own right, with a $1b-plus annual budget for scientific research and development. Some of its work is for national security (i.e., ways to detect and prevent bioterrorism). Some is designed for commercial use, including work on clean energy and public health. The Hanford site and PNNL thus remain central to the Tri-Cities economy. But much less so than in the 1980s, when the plant's closure was imminent. Today, the region's dependence on federal dollars, in terms of jobs and wages, is roughly half what it was then, according to Karl Dye of Tridec, the area's economic development council. That's thanks to the rise of other sectors including agriculture (potatoes, apples, sweet corn, grapes, etc.), food processing, tourism, transportation, construction and of course education and health (you'll find that everywhere). When the Hanford nuclear site closed, a modern nuclear plant opened nearby, which still provides power today. It's in fact the only commercial nuclear plant in Washington state operating currently, and one of just 93 nationwide. The fact that Washington state doesn't have a corporate or personal income tax surely helps draw companies and retirees to the Tri-Cities, fueling some of its rapid growth. Amazon will soon open two new 1m-square-foot warehouses in the area. The port of Pasco, along with the BNSF and Union Pacific railroads, help move agricultural and industrial goods to Pacific gateways and onto export markets like Asia. Tri-Cities is certainly feeling the national labor shortage, notably in its agricultural sector. It's also experiencing the national run-up in housing prices, making it difficult to accommodate newcomers eager to fill open jobs. Another specific labor challenge is a wave of retirements among engineers, scientists and other professionals employed at Hanford and PNNL. They're not easily replaced.

NANTUCKET, MASSACHUSETTES

March 2022

"Call Me Ishmael." So reads the opening line of Moby Dick, one of America's most famous works of fiction. There's nothing fictitious though, about the whaling profession central to the novel's plot. Ishmael's seafaring takes him to far corners of the earth hunting for sperm whales, starting his journey in Nantucket, an island off the coast of Massachusetts. Just as Houston is today's capital of petroleum-based oil, Nantucket was the booming capital of the whale oil industry in the early 1800s. Long before kerosene lamps and later light bulbs, oil from sperm whales proved ideal for illumination, burning bright and without any foul odors. Whale oil was prized for candle making as well, and as a lubricating liquid useful for maintaining the young country's growing stock of industrial machinery. At the time of America's founding, Nantucket was its 12th most populous city, thanks to jobs associated with whaling. As late as 1820, it was still in the top 20. Like nearly all booming economies throughout U.S. history, Nantucket and its whaling industry depended on immigrant labor, often from the Portuguese world where seafaring helped build a global empire (there's a reason why places from Brazil to Angola speak Portuguese today). Many seafarers came from Africa's Cape Verde islands—Nantucket is still home to a large ethnic Cape Verdean community today. One of Moby Dick's main characters, in fact, is a sailor from West Africa. Another is from the South Pacific. Still another is of Indian descent (as in the country India). Another is Native American, a group that originally settled Nantucket. Collectively, their labor helped build some of the largest family fortunes of the day, not to mention large mansions, some of which still stand. Others, however, perished from a major fire that destroyed much of Nantucket in 1846. By then, the island's whaling economy was already in decline, peaking in the 1830s. The 1840s, as it happened, brought a better opportunity for shipowners: Sailing people to San Francisco to participate in the California gold rush (construction of the transcontinental railroad was still a few decades away). Nantucket by this time was already losing some whaling business to nearby New Bedford, whose port was better suited for larger and longer-range vessels increasingly dominating the industry. According to the National Park Service website: *"In 1823, New Bedford passed Nantucket in the number of whaleships departing annually on voyages, and never gave up its lead. With the arrival of the railroad in 1840 and easier access to New York and Boston markets, New Bedford became the wealthiest city in the world."* Nantucket's whaling industry—along with its economy—then suffered additional setbacks with Confederate raids on whaling ships during the Civil War (Nantucket was a center of Quaker opposition to slavery and this unloved by Confederates). Then, the biggest blow of all, not just to Nantucket's economy but the entire whaling industry: In 1859, Edwin Drake struck oil in western Pennsylvania, ushering in the age of hydrocarbons. No need for whale oil to light homes anymore. And so, whaling—as a major U.S. industry anyway—passed into history. A 2008 article in the New York Times captures its legacy: *"Whaling, after all, was one of the world's first great multinational businesses, a global enterprise of audacious reach and import. From the 1700s through the mid-1800s, oil extracted from the blubber of whales and boiled in giant pots gave light to America and much of the Western world. The United States whaling fleet peaked in 1846 with 735 ships out of 900 in the world. Whaling was the fifth-largest industry in the United States; in 1853 alone, 8,000 whales were slaughtered for whale oil shipped to light lamps around the world, plus sundry other parts used in hoop skirts, perfume, lubricants and candles."* So whaling went away. But what happened to Nantucket? Its economy unsurprisingly suffered decades of decline. The island's Wikipedia entry uses the words "underdeveloped" and "isolated." Until, that is, the mid-1900s, when real estate developers began restoring old properties and marketing the island as a summer getaway for New England's elite. The efforts worked, and Nantucket today is America's most expensive market for vacation homes, according to a 2019 report by the National Association of Realtors. Around 15,000 people live on the island year-round, a sharp increase from even ten years ago. During summers—August especially—the population swells to more like 50,000. According to Zillow, average home values now exceed $2.1m, up 17% y/y (the average price in San Francisco by contrast is $1.5m). Nantucket has thus reclaimed its spot among the country's wealthiest places, but more quietly than during its whaling days of global commercial significance. High-end tourism, not whaling, is now the top industry, along with money earned from seasonal residents. Some of the money, no doubt, descends from generations past, bequeathed by family fortunes from whaling. Not the Kennedy family though. Its first members moved from Ireland to Massachusetts just as whaling was in its waning days—President Kennedy's father would grow rich by (among other endeavors) investing in Hollywood movies. The Kennedys, however, made their home in Cape Cod, not Nantucket. Another presidential family visits frequently though: The Bidens have long spent their Thanksgivings on the island. They did so this past fall, highlighting a recovery in arrivals as the pandemic recedes. The crisis was costly for many of the island's restaurants, shops, hotels and art galleries, not to mention its whaling museum. But airport traffic last August was almost back to pre-crisis levels, aided by an increase in remote workers. Some locals aren't happy about the influx, calling for a ban on short-term vacation rentals. But a referendum on the matter failed last year, opposed by owners of real estate earning lots of money by renting out their homes through platforms like Airbnb. The issue has become a hot topic in many tourist economies across the country, tying in with concerns about affordable housing for local teachers, firefighters, police officers, electricians, plumbers and the like. But a much larger problem looms for Nantucket. A Zillow study in 2017 estimated that $1.8b worth of Nantucket real estate (it's worth a lot more today) lies on land projected to eventually be under water—literally. Climate change, in other words, is becoming a whale of a problem.

CHEYENNE, WYOMING

March 2022

Sixty years ago, as the Cuban Missile Crisis threatened humanity's existence, President John F. Kennedy thankfully decided not to fire. But if he did, a group of highly-trained U.S. Air Force personnel in Wyoming were ready. In 2022, the U.S. and Russia are again adversaries, and once again, there's unnerving talk about using nuclear weapons. Also once again, the folks in Wyoming are ready. Just in case. Cheyenne, Wyoming, specifically, is home to the F.E. Warren Air Force Base, a critical node in America's nuclear defense. It's one of three bases—the others are in North Dakota and Montana—equipped with underground silos capable of firing nuclear-armed Minutemen III ICBMs (intercontinental ballistic missiles). The base also happens to be central to Cheyenne's *economy*, alongside state government. Wyoming, as it happens, is a relatively young state, and today the least populous of any state. Like many cities of the Great Plains and Rocky Mountains, it owes its existence to the first transcontinental railroad, completed in 1869. Two years earlier, the Union Pacific railroad chose present-day Cheyenne as a base of operations, roughly 1,000 miles west of Chicago and 1,000 miles east of San Francisco. A U.S. army base—on the site of what's today the Air Force base—was established there as well. When Wyoming became a state, Cheyenne became its capital. The "Cowboy and Indian" culture of American lore soon developed, tied to the cattle trade. Cheyenne was briefly a major airline hub in the early days of aviation. Today, Wyoming is the country's largest coal producer thanks to reserves in the Powder River Basin. Alongside agriculture and energy is tourism, the third leg of the state's economy today. Wyoming is, after all, home to Yellowstone National Park, not to mention Jackson Hole, an affluent resort that hosts an important Federal Reserve event each summer. Grand Teton National Park is in Wyoming as well. But these sites are in the mountainous northwest corner of the state. Cheyenne, in the southeast corner, is in flat country, lacking any natural wonders to attract tourists. Instead, it lures them with its cowboy and Native American culture, celebrated each year at Frontier Days, a ten-day event that attracted 550,000 people last summer—the event was canceled the year before due to Covid. The University of Wyoming, in nearby Laramie, also has a major impact on the Cheyenne economy. Health care facilities, public schools and retailers like Walmart are major employers. So still, incidentally, is Union Pacific. Hardly just focused on its railroading past, however, Wyoming, including Cheyenne, is now trying to become a hub for the crypto-economy. Favorable laws and regulations are attracting crypto organizations like Kraken (an exchange), Cardano (a smart contract platform) and Ripple Labs (payment solutions). That's controversial in some circles, but not as controversial as the state's financial secrecy laws, allegedly making it a haven for tax avoidance. This came to light with the Pandora Papers, a collection of leaked documents that prompted the Washington Post to write an article entitled: "The 'Cowboy Cocktail': How Wyoming Became One of the World's Top Tax Havens." For all its financial ambitions, military might and clout in state politics, Cheyenne remains a small city with just 100,000 people in the metro area—roughly 15,000 are associated with the Air Force base, including military retirees and their families. That 100,000 figure makes it about the same size as Grand Forks, North Dakota, or Hot Springs, Arkansas. Its population did grow a healthy 8% during the 2010s, boosted by the residual impact of Denver's mega-boom just an hour-and-a-half to the south. Between Denver and Cheyenne is Fort

Collins, Colorado, where population rose a scorching 19% last decade. Will the growth continue to bleed north and ultimately turn Cheyenne into a boom town? Not having an attractive mountain landscape like Denver or Jackson Hole hurts. Housing prices have nevertheless been rising sharply, though that's been true almost everywhere during the pandemic. The current jump in energy and ag prices certainly helps Wyoming. The state is one of nine without an income tax, which can be both a magnet for new residents but an obstacle to development projects, including plans to revitalize downtowns, improve broadband access or attract new air service. Of course, Wyoming's distaste for public taxing and spending belies Cheyenne's economic dependence on federal military dollars and state government. As for Warren Air Force base, the military originally armed it with ICBMs in the 1950s because of its location in the center of the country yet far enough north to strike the Soviet Union over the North Pole. The Soviet Union is gone, but the missiles remain, ready again to defend the U.S... just in case.

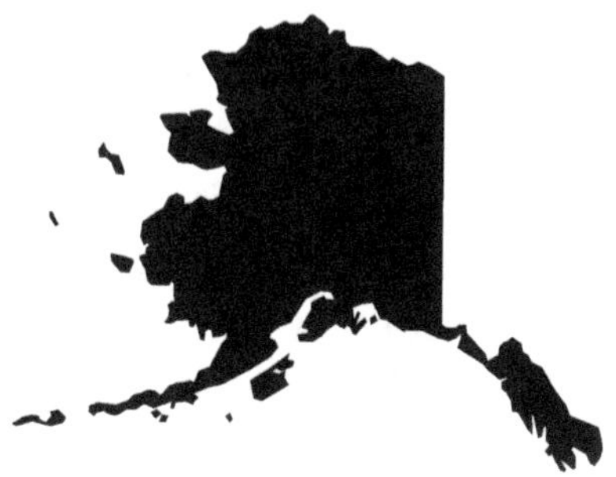

SITKA, ALASKA

March 2022

Long before tensions over Ukraine, long before the Cold War and long before even their alliance in World War II, the United States and Russia made a deal. It was 1867, a few years after the American Civil War, and a year after Russia's defeat in the Crimea War. The Russian Czar had war debts to pay. So he gladly accepted $7m in gold from the Americans, in exchange for the barren lands of Alaska, where Russians had established small settlements and fur-trading businesses. A grand "folly," some in the U.S. Congress said at the time. Even so, the deal was approved, and the transaction sealed on October 18, 1867. A ceremony was held in Russia's Alaskan capital: Sitka. Today, a Russian Orthodox church still stands in Sitka's city center, a rebuilt version of one originally constructed in the days of Russian rule. It's one of many reasons why 200,000 tourists were expected to visit in the summer of 2020—that is, before Covid mothballed the cruise industry. Most come for the stunning natural beauty and exotic wildlife. And come they will: Officials expect a record-breaking tourist season this summer. Like in nearby Juneau—also located amid the archipelago of islands stretching down the coast of southeastern Alaska—the Sitka economy involves a lot of seafood. The town is home to three large processing plants including Silver Bay Seafoods, the largest. It's also the base of hundreds of commercial vessels, most operated by self-employed commercial fishermen. The economics of the seafood industry aren't easy these days, not with competition from lower-wage countries like China, and Russia too before recent events. Labor at home is hard to come by, so the processing plants have long recruited from as far away as Asia, Latin America and Eastern Europe. They're in fact among the most prolific issuers of foreign H2-B visas authorized for temporary non-agricultural jobs. In 2019, non-Alaska residents (including seasonal workers from Seattle and elsewhere on the U.S. mainland) accounted for 34% of Sitka's workforce. According to the Sitka Economic Development Association, the city ranks as the 15th busiest seafood port in the U.S. based on value (major products include salmon, halibut and black cod). Sitka's single largest employer is the local hospital. Though the state capital moved to Juneau a few decades after the Russians left, government work is still a major component of Sitka's labor market. The U.S. Coast Guard and the U.S. Forest Service have sizeable footprints. Another notable employer is the Sitka Tribe of Alaska (STA), a federally recognized government entity representing Native peoples including the Tlingit tribe. The Tlingit have inhabited the area for thousands of years, at one point engaging in military conflict with Russia. The Census counts about 12% of Sitka's population as Native American. Roughly 8% are Asian and 7% Hispanic. Overall, the population of about 8,500 is shrinking and aging, a big reason for the seafood sector's labor shortage. One thing that's definitely *not* in short supply though, is fresh water and cheap hydropower. Is Sitka wealthy? It does have a rather high median household income of $82,000, compared to $78,000 for all of Alaska and $65,000 nationwide. Alaskan residents should get a big check next year thanks to high oil prices—the state redistributes much of its oil wealth to Alaskans through an annual dividend payment. Imagine, by the way, if Russia had kept Alaska. It would be an even larger oil power today, never mind all the Alaskan gold that was discovered a few years after the sale. Understatement of the century: That $7m sale turned out to be a pretty good deal for America. And one more thing about Sitka's history when it was still part of Russia; this is from the Sitka Economic Development Association:

"During the mid-1800s, Sitka, known as the 'Paris of the Pacific,' was the largest, most industrious city on the Pacific Rim, with Canton, China and San Francisco, California following behind. Ships from many nations visited the port. Furs, salmon, lumber and ice were exported to Hawaii, Mexico and California. There was an active shipyard and foundry."

HARPERS FERRY, WEST VIRGINIA

April 2022

There are no coal mines in this part of West Virginia. Instead, Harpers Ferry, located in the state's northeastern panhandle, is best known for an 1859 revolt against slavery. Today, much of the town's economy depends on visits from history-minded tourists, eager to see the site of John Brown's rebellion. Though quickly suppressed by the U.S. Army, the action triggered abolitionist sentiment and Southern unease, contributing to the outbreak of civil war in 1861. Harpers Ferry happens to be a picturesque little town in the Shenandoah Valley, all the more reason to visit. It overlooks the meeting of two prominent rivers—the Shenandoah and the Potomac—bordering both Virginia and Maryland. No, this is not Las Vegas- or Orlando-volume tourism here; just 300,000 or so arrivals in a good year, most from surrounding areas. The pandemic counterintuitively boosted tourism, at least in 2021, when 310,000 people visited Harpers Ferry National Historic Park (which includes a large swathe of land surrounding the town). That was up 3% from 2019 as Americans, during the Covid outbreak, favored car trips to nearby places rather than more distant trips by plane. Only a few hundred people actually live in Harpers

Ferry proper. Those employed in the tourist sector typically commute from nearby towns, including those elsewhere in Jefferson County, population 58,000. In 2020, the county had a per capita income of $55,000, high by West Virginia standards but a bit below the U.S. national average of $60,000. Average housing prices are lower, however. The current unemployment rate is just 2%, partly reflecting the health of local tourism. Nearly a third of Jefferson County's residents have at least a bachelor's degree, compared to just 23% for all of West Virginia. Other major employers include Shepherd University with roughly 3,000 students, a local casino, multiple wineries and distilleries, and of course schools and health care facilities. Europe's TeMa, which builds products for the construction sector, has a factory in the county. Giants Procter & Gamble and Clorox are in a neighboring county. Agriculture (wheat, soybeans, corn, etc.), warehousing and manufacturing complement the tourist sector. Federal agencies including the Departments of Homeland Security and Agriculture, as well as the Coast Guard, have facilities in the county too. Importantly, Harpers Ferry is less than 90 minutes by car from Washington, DC, making it a prime location for "super commuting," in other words combining remote work with occasional office visits. More convenient are commutes to the Virginia suburbs around Dulles airport, an area booming with defense contractors and IT firms. Dennis Jarvis of the Jefferson County Development Authority notes how 1.8m people live within a one-hour drive of the area, with commuters flowing both in and out. Amtrak and Maryland's MARC rail, as it happens, run daily trains from the center of town to Washington's Union station. This also makes it easy for Washington residents to come enjoy a day or two hiking around Harpers Ferry or learning about its intriguing history. That history, in fact, runs deeper than just Civil War-era events. Harpers Ferry first gained attention when President George Washington (you may have heard of him) selected it as one of two sites for a federal armory (the other was in Springfield, Mass.). For a time, it was an ideal place to build guns and many other industrial products thanks to the cheap hydropower provided by the town's two rivers. A canal, and later a railroad, facilitated movement of raw materials in and finished products out. Cheap labor came from Ireland and Germany. Harpers Ferry was thus one of America's earliest industrial hubs, featuring not just arms manufacturers but iron foundries, machine shops, sawmills, cotton mills, flour mills, tanneries, blacksmiths, woodworkers and wagon makers. That was before the 1860s. The Civil War would destroy much of the town's infrastructure. And efforts at post-war revival failed amid recurrent floods and droughts. The second half of the 19th century instead became an age of coal, steel, oil and large factory towns with armies of low-wage workers toiling for giant corporations—in places like Pittsburgh, not Harpers Ferry. During a later war—World War II—the U.S. established Harpers Ferry National Monument, later adding Storer College, a school built after the Civil War for newly freed slaves. Fast forward to 2022, and the eastern panhandle of West Virginia is the fastest-growing area in a state that overall saw population *shrink* during the 2010s. Jefferson County by contrast grew 7%, and neighboring Berkeley County double that. The contracting coal mine economy? Not in this part of West Virginia.

MINNEAPOLIS, MINNESOTA

April 2022

"The Silicon Valley of Food." That's one way someone once described Minnesota's Twin Cities, whose economic rise depended less on traditional manufacturing than many of its Midwestern peers. While Detroit was busy building cars, Pittsburgh busy building steel and Chicago busy building, well, pretty much everything, mills in Minneapolis and St. Paul were busy turning wheat from America's Great Plains into flour used for bread. From those humble roots emerged a 21st-century food processing powerhouse of global significance, not to mention an economy that in many ways looks more Sun Belt than Rust Belt. The Minneapolis metro area, which includes the adjacent city of St. Paul, is home to Cargill, an agricultural goliath with $134b in annual revenue. That makes it similar in size to Ford or General Motors, and larger than even JPMorgan Chase or Johnson & Johnson. Cargill, with 155,000 workers, is America's largest private company (in other words, the largest without publicly traded stock; it raises money by other means). Cargill, furthermore, is one of the four "ABCD" firms that dominate global agricultural commodity trading, the others being Archer Daniels Midland, Bunge and Dreyfuss. You might recognize other corporate manifestations of the Minneapolis industrial food complex, like General Mills (maker of Cheerios and Wheaties), Hormel (headquartered south of the city) and Land O'Lakes. There's the Minneapolis Grain Exchange. And there's CHS, an agribusiness giant indirectly owned by some 500,000 farmers and ranchers. The Twin Cities are also leaders in biotech innovation, which naturally has implications for food manufacturing (more commonly referred to as food processing). Food, however, is far from the only reason this economy gained weight. The Minneapolis economy is by any measure a successful economy, extremely well-diversified and unusually well-defended against recessions. These days, it's perhaps more renowned for health care than food, which served it well during the 2008-09 recession, which barely affected the health care sector. The pandemic of course was a crisis centered on health care, but one in which many health care companies nevertheless thrived. One was Minneapolis-based UnitedHealth, the country's largest health insurer and sixth largest U.S. company overall, behind only Walmart, Amazon, Apple, Berkshire Hathaway and CVS (based on annual revenues). Not too far from the metro area is Rochester, Minnesota, home of the famed Mayo Clinic. The largest employer in the Twin Cities is the Allina Health system, with a staff of nearly 30,000. Health Partners and Fairview Health are almost as large. According to the Minnesota Department of Employment and Economic Development, the area is home to more than 40 medical device manufacturers with at least 100 employees each. During the pandemic, local companies 3M and Medtronic were key suppliers of personal protective equipment (PPE) and ventilators, respectively. The story doesn't end with food and health care. The state-run University of Minnesota is located downtown along the Mississippi River. St. Paul is home to Minnesota's state government. The largest employer outside of health care, education and government is a familiar name to all Americans: Minneapolis-headquartered Target. Wells Fargo, though larger in San Francisco and Charlotte, has a giant presence in Minneapolis as well. US Bank, the nation's fifth-largest bank, is headquartered in the Twin Cities. So is the retailer Best Buy and so is the trucking giant C.H. Robinson. Fastenal, a big industrial supplier, is based about two hours south in a town called Winona. In fact, the Twin Cities are home to 16 Fortune

500 companies, putting it in the same league as Atlanta and Washington, DC. It even attracts a decent amount of tourism, thanks to major sporting venues and the Mall of America, which pre-Covid attracted 40m visitors a year (the mall also employs more than 10,000 people). But what about information technology, a key engine of 21st-century economic growth? Yes, here too, Minneapolis is strong, benefitting like Silicon Valley, Boston and Los Angeles—if on a much smaller scale—from a legacy of Cold War-era defense contracts for various military supplies, computer products and scientific instruments. The area has an abundance of finance jobs too, some of which—like some IT jobs—cater to the health sector. No wonder why the Minneapolis metro today has the 28th highest per capita income in the country, out of the nearly 400 ranked by the Commerce Department. Though it ranked as high as the ninth-largest metro in America by population a century ago, it ranks a still-impressive 16 today, holding its place thanks to robust 9% population growth during the 2010s. That's high for a place not in the Sun Belt or Far West. It was certainly high compared to other cold-weather places like New York, Chicago, Philadelphia and Detroit. Minneapolis is a major international airline hub thanks to Delta. Unemployment was 3.1% before Covid and just 2.4% currently. The area's labor force participation rate is 72%, compared to 63% nationally. It did lose manufacturing jobs during the 2000s like the rest of the country, but even during the 2008-09 recession, it added nearly 8,000 new health care and education jobs annually, similar to the gains *before* the recession. This gave rise to the term "Minneapolis Miracle," still relevant given conditions in 2021. So is there anything negative to say about the Minneapolis economy? Well, labor shortages are pretty severe, holding back further expansion. The region's extremely cold winters don't help when attracting newcomers, and many people given the choice to work from home would rather do so in places without the need to shovel snow. Sure enough, the population shrank slightly in the 12 months to July 2021. Perhaps most worrying are the challenges the Twins Cities have faced in fostering economic opportunities for historically disadvantaged groups. It's of course a challenge not unique to Minneapolis, but one that burst into national attention there with George Floyd's fatal encounter with Minneapolis police officers. Also key to the

future health of the economy is the area's immigrant population, which accounted for 16% of the Minneapolis-St. Paul labor force in 2019, according to the New American Economy. Large immigrant groups include Somalis, Ethiopians, Mexicans and the Hmong community from southeast Asia. To be clear, Minneapolis never gained the immense economic scale of Chicago or even Detroit. But nor did it experience as difficult a transition from the industrial economy to the knowledge economy. Likewise, Minneapolis never became quite a global superstar city like Chicago in the 2020s, owing to the domestic orientation of its top industries like food and health care, along with its relatively sleepy downtown. Nothing wrong with that though, as the Minneapolis Miracle makes clear.

(6 1)

NAVAJO NATION

April 2022

America's largest Indian reservation is larger in fact than ten states—16m acres. But it doesn't have a single Walmart. Not one. And the reason goes a long way toward explaining why the economies of Native American lands are so difficult to develop. Navajo Nation, whose reservation lies in the "Four Corners" region of the U.S. west, overlaps with four states: Arizona, Utah, New Mexico and Colorado. But not all Navajos (sometimes called Diné) live on the reservation. In fact, fewer than half do, owing to limited economic opportunities. The number is about 174,000, according to the Census. That's roughly the size of Abilene, TX, or Bloomington, IL. Like many of America's 300-plus Indian reservations, the one governed by Navajo Nation suffers from extreme poverty and underdevelopment. According to the Nation's President, Jonathan Nez, writing in the Washington Post last year, 40% of the reservation's residents lack running water while 27% of homes lack electricity, let alone broadband. Some 80% of the area's roads are unpaved. Fewer than a tenth of residents have a college degree. The unemployment rate between 2013 and 2017 averaged close to 20%. Rates of alcoholism, suicide and domestic violence are high. Covid hit hard.

Unlike the Cheyenne River Reservation, for example, Navajo Nation does possess valuable natural resources including oil, gas and coal. Revenues from these resources, combined with federal aid, help fund a tribal government that operates various business enterprises, including a power company, an energy exploration and production company, a network of gas stations, a casino operator, a power utility, and so on. Public employment, including jobs with the Federal Bureau of Indian Affairs (BIA) and the Indian Health Service, dominates the reservation's labor market. Some residents earn a living as artisans or service workers. Local flea markets are popular places to buy and sell items. The reservation attracts some tourists, often driving through on road trips. There's enough of an economy, no doubt, to support a Walmart. Sure enough, Navajo residents routinely shop at Walmart and other familiar retail establishments… but not in reservation towns—not even in the Navajo capital of Window Rock. Instead, they cross the border to shop, in towns like Gallup, NM, and Flagstaff, AZ. Albuquerque is a roughly three-hour drive from Window Rock. Phoenix is about seven hours. Walmart and other businesses, simply put, are averse to managing the legal complexities and liabilities associated with tribal law, which coexists with U.S. law. This in turn deprives the Navajo Nation of valuable tax income. Real estate law is one area of complexity that often proves a barrier to development. President Nez, for his part, lays some of the blame on Washington, specifically the (BIA), which is charged with delivering government funding and services to tribal areas. He said the BIA "strangles us in red tape anytime we attempt to improve conditions on our lands." An example is the multiple layers of approval required for development projects and having to deal, more generally, with multiple overlapping government bodies. As Nez said in a recent address: "We are, by far, the most over-regulated population in this country." Banks are certainly deterred, often unwilling to do home loans or construction loans because tribal land is held in trust by Washington so can't be used as collateral. Most Navajo residents live on rented land or in government housing. Small businesses and Navajo entrepreneurs are further challenged by underdeveloped transportation, utility and communication infrastructure. With education achievement low, employers have to hire many non-Navajo workers for higher-skilled jobs. The Navajo tribal government itself, the reservation's largest employer, says 70% of its contracted work goes to non-Navajo businesses, with much of the compensation spent *off* the reservation. In 2019, tribal revenues dropped sharply following the closure of a coal-fired power plant long operated by Peabody, the country's largest coal company. A nearby mine was closed as well, reducing Navajo Nation's revenues by an estimated $30m to $50m a year, according to President Nez. The Covid crisis naturally hurt casino and tourism revenue. On the other hand, Covid-related stimulus payments, as well as money from Washington's infrastructure bill, offer a fiscal windfall. Nevertheless, Navajo Nation still depends greatly on taxes and royalties from natural resource development, prompting a push to diversify. Working with Four Corners Economic Development, it's contemplating a freight railway that would connect the reservation to BNSF's main east-west line running through the U.S. Southwest. Last year, the medical glove manufacturer Rhino Health expanded its production capacity in Navajo Nation. Interestingly, the tribal government came close to buying the bankrupt gun manufacturer Remington in 2020. It's now investing in clean energy projects including solar and wind. Helium extraction is likewise viewed as an opportunity. Some think legalizing cannabis sales would provide a meaningful boost. As for the economy today, Derrick Watchman, formerly CEO of Navajo Nation Gaming Enterprise and currently president of the tribal advisory firm Sagebrush Hill, estimates the reservation's total GDP to be something around $8b to $10b. Enough to support a Walmart? Absolutely.

KANSAS CITY, MISSOURI

April 2022

A sleepy midwestern town? That might be its reputation today, fairly or unfairly. But that was certainly not the case a century ago. During the prohibition-era of the 1920s, and even into the Depression years of the 1930s, Kansas City was more associated with adjectives like sinful, sketchy, edgy and perhaps what we'd today call Las Vegas-like. There's a reason why Wilbert Harrison went there to chase women and wine, as "Kanas City," his number one hit song from 1959 recounts (go look for it on YouTube). America's most geographically central metro started out like many cities on the western lands once owned by France—as a place to trade furs. It is, after all, located where the Missouri and Kansas Rivers meet, quite conveniently for river commerce. When the railroads came and expanded after the Civil War, Kansas City boomed, becoming a mini-Chicago of sorts. It was number two behind Chicago in meatpacking, for example, and likewise served as a commercial hub for surrounding farm products—a place to buy and sell grains and seeds and animals, etc. It also, less welcomingly, mimicked some of Chicago less-flattering characteristics, including government corruption and organized crime. Amid a wave of impoverished European immigrants, one family's arrival from Ireland would shape the city for decades. The Pendergasts, led by brothers Jim and later Tom, built one of America's most powerful urban political machines, on par with the Dailey machine in Chicago or Tammany Hall in New York City. In the meantime, by the early 1900s, Black Americans eager to escape the south rode the rails and busses northward in search of better lives. Amid these migrants were many musicians from New Orleans, destined to turn Kansas City into one of the great Jazz capitals of America. The Pendergast machine, working closely with organized criminal syndicates, made sure the nightclubs and gambling dens were open, and that the alcohol flowed freely, even during the Prohibition years. Gambling. Seedy nightclubs. You get the picture. It's much different to be sure, than today's image of Kansas City. Post-World War II suburbanization changed its downtown character, robbing it of its vibrancy until some measures of revival more recently. It's never experienced an urban renaissance like Chicago though, in part because it simply doesn't have the scale to be a global commercial and tourist hub. What it does have is a fairly diverse economy with an above-average number of professionals for its size. It's still a leading transportation hub, with more rail traffic than anywhere but Chicago. That's unsurprising given its geographic centrality, which makes it a major trucking hub as well. It punches below its weight in air traffic, however, owing to its limited tourism and modest size (it's the country's 35th largest metro by population). But its aviation heft should improve with the modernization of its airport now underway. That alone is a project providing lots of construction jobs. Kansas City is attracting more than its fair share of new facilities typical of the 21st century U.S. economy, including call centers, health facilities and especially warehouses. Meta, owner of Facebook, is building an $800m data center. Kansas City, which straddles the states of Missouri and Kansas, has plenty of prosperous suburbs, major league baseball and football franchises and decent population growth (7% during the 2010s). Though neither a state capital nor home to a large university, the area has one of the largest federal government workforces (non-military) outside of Washington. The IRS alone has nearly 5,000 workers in Kansas City. After Uncle Sam, the largest metro area employer is a hospital, followed by Cerner, a health care technology firm with nearly

$6b in revenue last year. Hallmark, H&R Block and the investment firm American Century are other familiar corporate names with Kansas City headquarters. Thanks in part to its distributional and logistic advantages, the area is home to major GM and Ford auto plants. The Ford plant is in fact one of the country's largest, building the company's most popular product, the F-150 pickup (that's actually the top selling vehicle in the U.S.). Honeywell, an aerospace giant, is helping to modernize the country's nuclear weapons at its Kansas City facilities. Grain and livestock processing, an old staple from the city's past, remains important today (the local baseball team got its name from an annual livestock show called the American Royal). The city likewise remains home to one of 12 Federal Reserve banks across the country (oddly enough, nearby St. Louis, Missouri, has one too). Kansas City officials do express some concern about mergers that have swallowed some prominent corporate citizens, including Sprint (purchased by T-Mobile) and DST Systems (purchased by SS&C). A Canadian railroad is now buying Kansas City Southern, though their combined network (assuming the merger is approved) could boost the city's stature as a gateway for traffic moving between Mexico and Canada. There have been some high-profile factory closures in recent years, including those by Harley Davidson and Procter and Gamble. In sum, Kansas City has a solid economy with solid population growth, outperforming other midwestern cities that peaked in national prominence during the first half of the 20th century. But it's certainly not a growth superstar in the vein of say, Austin, Nashville, Charlotte or Denver. The nickname "Paris of the Plains" sounds a bit hyperbolic. But better that, surely, than being the subject of songs about sin.

(6 3)

SUSANVILLE, CALIFORNIA

May 2022

The history will sound familiar. Like so many towns in the American West, people originally came for the mining, the farming and the logging. Today, however, the people of Susanville, a town in remote northeastern California, depend for their livelihoods on something altogether different, a local industry, in fact, facing a major crisis. This is not the California you see on T.V. No Hollywood movie stars. No billion-dollar tech startups. No cutting-edge aerospace companies, tourist-filled beaches or world-class farmland. The economy in Susanville revolves around just one thing: Prisons. Three of them in fact, two run by the state of California and one by the Federal government. One of the state facilities, however— the California Correctional Center (CCC)—is slated for closure in June. It's part of the state's plan to cut $172m from its $14b prison budget. And it reflects a national trend to reverse a decades-long surge in the number of incarcerated Americans. Susanville's economy, as a result, faces ruin. The three prisons provide roughly half of the town's employment. And much of the other half—local government, retail, health care, etc.—depends on the incomes of prison workers. Even the local community college gets by with significant enrollment from Susanville's prisoners. A documentary about the town produced by "No Way Back" profiled a small business owner with a contract to provide milk and other dairy products to the prisons. With all of this now threatened by the CCC closure, Susanville's real estate values are plummeting. Residents with the means are leaving, accelerating a long-run population drop reflective of declines throughout rural America—Susanville saw its non-prisoner population shrink 14% in the 2010s. The prison population, meanwhile, is about 6,000. There's a small Indian Reservation in the middle of town, where the tribal government runs a modest casino and hotel. There's a Walmart in town too. But the best-paid jobs are those in the prisons, specifically prison guards represented by one of California's most powerful unions, the California Correctional Peace Officers Association. With two large prisons remaining after CCC's closure, Susanville will still have plenty of state and federal money flowing in. But it seems inevitable that the economy will shrink sharply from its current level. A once-vibrant sawmill industry is long gone, with the last mill closing in 2004. The town's efforts to reinvent itself are challenged by the area's remoteness, and the fact that just 6% of residents over 25 have college degrees. Reno, a booming economy across the border in Nevada, is 1.5 hours away by car, making it a difficult daily commute. Sacramento, California's capital, is 3.5 hours away. Still another threat to Susanville: Destructive fires and droughts. As for basic local services like police and fire protection, the town has some breathing room thanks to the American Rescue Plan Act that Congress passed last year. ARPA, officials say, "provides the city with some time to research revenue increasing or cost saving items that may preserve the city's ability to provide the vital services at the level our citizens are accustomed." But it adds "the City's General Fund financial situation is serious, and the city cannot continue to operate at its current service levels unless revenues increase."

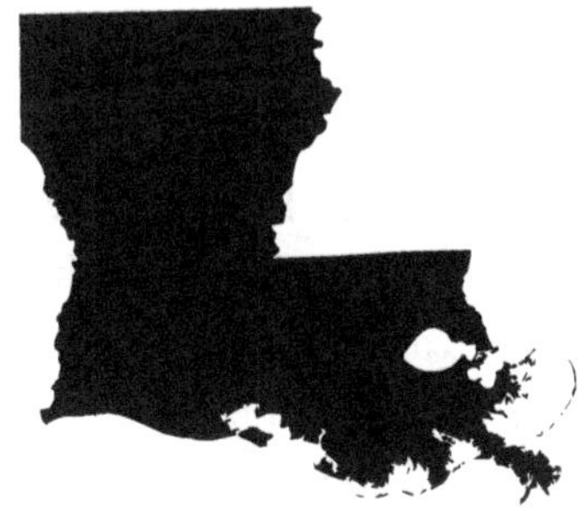

LAKE CHARLES, LOUSIANA

May 2022

The ingenuity of mankind. The wrath of Mother Nature. In the swampy marshlands of southwest Louisiana, both are on full display. Lake Charles, a town of about 210,000 people about two hours east of Houston, isn't the most likely place for multi-billion-dollar engineering projects. In the early 20th century, intrepid teams of geologists came to this remote area seeking oil, braving snakes, leeches and alligators. Sure enough, they found what they were looking for, transforming Louisiana's economy in the process. Today, Lake Charles is a place of great importance to America's energy sector, attracting a massive $110b in capital investments between 2012 and 2020, according to McKinsey Consulting. That's like the entire economy of Ecuador. Another $22b worth of projects are under-way, says R.B. Smith of the Southwest Louisiana Economic Development Alliance. And billions more are pending. Along the waterways connecting Lake Charles to the Gulf of Mexico stand elaborate feats of engineering, many focused on turning crude oil into gasoline, chemicals, plastics and other materials essential to modern life. The area is home to the seventh largest U.S. oil refinery, owned by Venezuela's Citgo. And most excitingly these days, Lake Charles has become ground zero for liquefied natural gas, or LNG. As early as 1981, the city opened its first LNG *import* terminal. By the 2010s, however, the fracking revolution turned America's natural gas shortage into a surplus, prompting a conversion of such terminals into *export* facilities. There are now three such facilities in Lake Charles. And plans for more are gaining momentum following Russia's invasion of Ukraine. With gas supplies to Europe disrupted and prices soaring, the last few months have seen a surge in LNG activity, with companies like Cheniere and Energy Transfer signing giant new deals with foreign buyers. Just last week, a Bloomberg News headline read: "U.S. LNG Deals Surge With 30% of Planned Export Capacity Sold." Earnings calls from natural gas and pipeline firms are now filled with mentions of Lake Charles. The LNG plants typically have their own shipping docks. But the Port of Lake Charles—used for shipping chemicals, petroleum products, forestry products and agricultural goods—is currently America's 12th busiest by tonnage. Lake Charles was founded during the Civil War, getting a boost when Louisiana's large forestry sector—a staple of its early economy—provided much of the lumber that rebuilt the South once the war was over. As mentioned, the area became a point of interest for oil explorers in the 1920s and 1930s. During World War II, as the port's website explains, *"firms such as Continental Oil, Cities Service, Firestone, Pittsburgh Plate Glass, Davison Chemical, Dresser Minerals, Citcon, Hercules, Conalco, Certainteed and others, built plants along the Calcasieu River in the Lake Charles area. Ships lined up at the docks to load rice, lumber, walnuts, tires, resin, cotton and numerous other products."* Rice was in fact another staple of the state's early economy, with both lumber and rice remaining important today—a Canadian company will in fact open a new lumber mill, reversing years of such mills leaving the U.S. In modern times, Lake Charles has also developed a rather large tourist sector, drawing visitors—many from booming Houston—to its five major casinos, one of them operated by a local Native American tribe. An old Air Force base, shuttered in the 1960s, has become a thriving base for aircraft maintenance and painting. As in pretty much every U.S. town, health care and public schools account for a substantial portion of local jobs. There's McNeese State University as well, along with a community college that helps train future workers in the aviation and hospitality sectors. With so much infrastructure investment, construction jobs are abundant. So there you have it: A giant petrochemical industry, the LNG capital of America, billions in new engineering projects, a thriving maritime port, a reviving forestry sector, strength in aviation and tourism… Lake Charles surely must be among America's fastest growing metro areas. Actually… There's sadly more to the story, and it involves Mother Nature. To be sure, GDP in the Lake Charles metro significantly outgrew the national average between 2013 and 2018. It will likely grow at an impressive pace in 2022, thanks to the current energy boom. Nevertheless, the economy is still smaller today than it was before its 2005 peak. 2005! In September of that year, less than a month after Hurricane Katrina brought havoc to New Orleans, Hurricane Rita smashed into Lake Charles, causing the economy of Calcasieu Parish to contract by nearly a fifth. Only around 2013 did things start turning up. And then: Devastation that made Rita seem like a picnic. The year 2020 was a nightmare for the whole world. In Lake Charles though, because of its heavy energy and tourism exposure, the economic carnage from Covid was magnified—21,300 jobs lost in April 2020 alone. This was just the start. In August, Hurricane Laura swept through, causing an estimated $12b in damage across southwestern Louisiana and Texas. Just six weeks later, it was Hurricane Delta's turn to deliver misery. McKinsey's study of the economy estimates that roughly half of all homes in Calcasieu Parish were damaged by the two storms. That's about 44,000 homes. Much of the population thus still lives in exile, waiting as houses are rebuilt. But rebuilding isn't easy in a nation currently suffering a labor shortage and ill-inclined to lift legal immigration. In the 12 months to July 2021, Lake Charles lost a larger percentage of people than any other U.S. metro. Keep in mind, despite its energy riches, Lake Charles is rife with poverty, featuring average incomes well below the national average, especially within the city itself and especially among Black residents, often living apart from Whites. Black Louisianans account for roughly a quarter of the parish's population, and about half of the city's population. Just 3% to 4% of area residents are Hispanic. Even fewer are of Asian descent or foreign born. The New York Times in 2006 described Lake Charles thus: "[a] coastal region of trailer parks, mangled sheds from last year's hurricanes and lonely roads built on top of canals that separate one swamp from another and gas rigs from streams full of crabs." Growth during the 2010s surely brought a degree of modernization and improved standards of living. But 2020 was a huge setback. Encouragingly, 2021 saw a jump in net job gains, notwithstanding yet another strike from nature, this time a tornado. And 2022 has brought LNG to the center stage of geopolitics, thrusting southwest Louisiana into economic prominence. It's an area of America, to be sure, stricken with severe income disparities and violent natural disasters, along with heavy pollution tied to the petrochemical industry. But it's no less a land of engineers, scientists and billion-dollar infrastructure, creating products essential to America's $24 trillion economy.

(65)

WASHINGTON, DISTRICT OF COLUMBIA

May 2022

The 1990s? Terrible. The first two decades of the 2000s? Miraculous. The 2020s? They're not looking good. If the District of Columbia were a state, it would rank number one for population loss during the pandemic. In the 12 months to July 2021, D.C. lost nearly 3% of its entire population—this after growing 15% during the 2010s. In fact, it grew by the same percentage as even Florida last decade, trailing only Utah, Idaho, Nevada, Colorado, North Dakota and Texas (D.C. would have grown faster still, surely, had its housing been more affordable). The city's workforce is 7% smaller today than it was pre-pandemic, even as federal government jobs—which account for roughly a quarter of total employment—remain stable. During the first six months of the pandemic alone, according to the D.C. Policy Center, 17,000 residents fled the District, many to adjacent Virginia and Maryland suburbs. The city's outsized university sector hasn't proved an anchor of stability like Uncle Sam. George Washington University, the district's largest private-sector employer, cut hundreds of jobs during the pandemic. Georgetown, Howard, American, Gallaudet and Catholic Universities faced difficult times as well with Covid canceling classes. In 2019, nearly 25m people visited D.C., making tourism another staple of the local economy. With Covid, much of *that* disappeared. Crime is on the rise. Many downtown offices remain vacant. And extremely high housing prices have dropped only modestly. Across the U.S., there's no economy with a history quite like Washington's. Its past, like its present, was shaped by politics—the city was originally founded as a political compromise: Alexander Hamilton gets to realize his plan to federalize state debts; Thomas Jefferson and James Madison get the federal capital located near their home state Virginia. Two decades later, during the War of 1812, the new city was ransacked and burned by the British army. Alexandria, a slave trading town originally part of D.C., voted to return to Virginia roughly a decade before the Civil War. For decades after the war, the federal government remained a rather small institution, restraining Washington's growth. But that changed after the New Deal during the 1930s, when the city's population soared. Federal expansion also gave birth to a large ecosystem of government contractors, lawyers, lobbyists, trade associations, international organizations, foreign embassies, think tanks, labor unions and the like. Highway construction, housing policies and racial tensions led to a suburban exodus in the 1960s and '70s, no different than what many U.S. cities experienced. Unlike other big cities, however, Washington never experienced de-industrialization, for the simple reason that it never had a manufacturing economy. Nor did it have a seaport, which was a major source of employment and economic activity in the other four major northeastern cities, namely Boston, New York, Philadelphia and Baltimore. Washington's economy nevertheless suffered terribly in the early 1990s recession. The D.C. Policy Center estimates that the city lost 63,000 jobs between 1990 and 1997, almost a tenth of total employment. During the same period, population shrank 12%. The city's local government became infamous for scandals and overspending, personified by a famously crack-smoking mayor named Marion Barry. In 1997, local officials ceded control of city finances to a federally-created control board, which set about to cut a $722m budget deficit. Its efforts were successful, aided by a booming national economy and a new generation of highly-educated young Americans eager to live in dense urban cities. All the while, the federal government continued to grow, even through the severe recession of 2008-09, which affected Washington much less than it did other places. D.C. was in fact one of only three "states" (along with Alaska and North Dakota) where total employment was higher at the end of 2010 than it was at the end of 2007. Following the recession, the city's population continued to spike. Same for its tax base, its tourist arrivals and—less welcomingly—its housing prices. Washington, indeed, joined the ranks of America's "Superstar Cities," buttressed by a suburban periphery that was likewise booming. Today, Washington is America's most educated city, with a third of all workers holding a graduate degree. The median salary for federal workers? $112,000. Washington was also America's largest city in which the majority of residents are Black. And while the Black population has dipped below the 50% mark, the District remains a major center of African-American culture and commerce. It has a thriving LGBTQ community as well. The city is now 11% Hispanic, while 13% of residents are foreign-born. But has Washington's two decades of prosperity come to an end? Has the pandemic ushered in a replay of the dismal 1990s? For Yesmin Sayin, who runs the D.C. Policy Institute, the single biggest concern is remote work. That's weakening the links, she said, between where people live and where people work. And in D.C. historically, the leading reason why people have moved to the city is because of their jobs. Remote work thus helps explain why the city is hemorrhaging people. The federal government, of course, remains a bastion of economic steadiness, notwithstanding occasional periods of fiscal austerity (i.e., the sequestration years of the early 2010s). Hospitals and local government are other stable employers. Universities are normalizing and tourism is reviving. But the large professional sector—including lawyers, regulators and so on that work for Uncle Sam—are increasingly electing to live outside the city. In turn, the service sector businesses catering to these workers—restaurants, coffee shops, hair salons, etc.—continue to suffer. Forget about Republican or Democrat. The future of Washington's economy may come down to Work from Home or Work from Office.

NORTH PLATTE, NEBRASKA

May 2022

You never know where an economy might spring to life. Even, perhaps, on the isolated Great Plains of Nebraska. Warren Buffett, the most famous Nebraskan, joked at the latest Berkshire Hathaway shareholder meeting: "In 1789, [imagine] you'd asked Ben Franklin, or somebody that was walking out of the Constitutional Convention, 'What do you think the prospects are for Nebraska?' His point is that there *was no state of Nebraska* in 1789, and there wouldn't be for another three quarters of a century. It became a state only after the Civil War, when more and more Americans sought new lives in the wild west—to farm its fertile land and make use of its abundant natural resources. Doing so became much easier with the buildout of railroads, most famously the first transcontinental railroad—built by Union Pacific and Central Pacific—connecting Iowa to northern California. Towns were born along the route, none more critical to the railroad's operation than North Platte in remote central Nebraska. Trains Magazine, citing historian David Howard Bain, described it as a winter camp for the railroad's workers, along with the miners, traders, Mormon emigrants, and stagecoach drivers passing through. To service them, "storekeepers, saloon owners, gamblers and brothel operators swarmed in." Another arrival was the entertainer "Buffalo Bill" Cody, helping to popularize the lore of the West. And so was born a classic western railroad town, sustained economically by the Union Pacific. More Americans would come to know North Platte during World War II, when it was a major stopping point for soldiers moving by rail across the country. By then there were automobiles, of course. And after the war, construction of the interstate highway system made long-distance passenger rail journeys increasingly uncommon. Nevertheless, shipping freight by rail remained economically competitive with trucks, even more so across long distances. So Union Pacific, in 1948, built the world's largest railcar yard in the world, a distinction it still holds today. Indeed, 155 years after first setting up shop in North Platte, Union Pacific remains its largest employer—more than 2,000 mostly well-paid union jobs, in a town of just 23,000 people total. Bailey Yard, as it's called, handles some 14,000 railcars every 24 hours, moving everything from agricultural products like corn and sugar to production inputs like coal, steel and chemicals. The yard handles automobiles too, and containers from Asia full of consumer goods. More unexpectedly, it's become a tourist site, providing North Platte with some economic diversification. But not enough, according to local leaders. The town remains remote, three hours west by car from Nebraska's largest city Omaha, and three hours northeast from Denver. Like many rural places across the U.S., North Platte is losing people, especially talented young people fleeing for better career opportunities—the town lost about 5% of its residents during the past decade. There's not much regular air service beyond a few United flights to Denver. Per capita income is less than $30,000. How to create more economic activity beyond the rail yard? There's actually one other major industry in rural Nebraska: Cattle. Lincoln County, home to North Platte, lies in one of the nation's top beef cattle-producing regions (Cherry County to its north, in fact, is number one nationwide). Local ranchers, however, must sell their animals to one of just four dominant meatpackers, namely Cargill, Tyson, JBS and National Beef. At a Congressional hearing last month, several independent cattle farmers accused the "Big Four" of acting in cartel-like fashion, driving down cattle prices and forcing more and more independent ranchers into bankruptcy.

It's the meatpackers who convert the livestock into a consumer product available at grocery stores. But farmers, who captured more than 70% of the final retail value in the 1970s, say they're capturing less than 40% today. Taking matters into their own hands, a group of Nebraska farmers is forming their own meatpacking enterprise based in (where else?) North Platte. Sustainable Beef, as the new venture calls itself, just received the town's blessing to build a beef processing plant with capacity to handle 1,500 cattle head per day. Construction should start this summer, taking roughly two years to complete. Not all of North Platte's residents are happy about the new plant. But others relish the chance to add hundreds of new jobs paying a starting wage of about $50,000 a year. And it's a new source of tax revenue to support schools and health facilities. Not stopping there, town officials are separately developing a new industrial park linked to Union Pacific's rail network. That will likely get the attention of manufacturers, who often want their production facilities along a rail line. Highway access is important too, which North Platte provides—Interstate 80 means both the east and west coasts are within a 24-hour truck journey. That was enough to convince Walmart to build a distribution site in North Platte. In the meantime, tourism is booming again, and Washington is increasingly eager to add more meatpacking capacity given shortages during the pandemic. The Biden Administration is also, incidentally, citing the meatpacking sector as an example of excessive consolidation, perhaps heralding some financial support for ventures like Sustainable Beef. The latter, no doubt, faces some difficult challenges even beyond waging a cattle battle with the financially muscular Big Four. Now is not a great time to be building a new plant, with construction and labor costs soaring. North Platte itself has the challenge of building enough additional housing to support the likely population growth associated with the new economic activity. Housing inventories are already scarce, says Cassie Condon of the North Platte Area Chamber of Commerce & Development Corporation. And so are available workers—the local unemployment rate is just 2.3%. What do you think the prospects are for North Platte, a contemporary Ben Franklin might ask? Perhaps on a track to beefier prosperity.

CHATTANOOGA, TENNESSEE

May 2022

t was bad. Really bad. During the 1980s, the industrial city of Chattanooga was—let's be blunt—a dying place. De-industrialization, more commonly associated with places like Detroit and Cleveland, was in full force. So was a flight to the suburbs. According to a Brookings Institution study, Chattanooga by 1990 was in "deep decline," having lost nearly 10% of its population during the 1960s, and another 10% between 1980 and 1990. Those declines refer to the city itself—surrounding suburbs, by contrast, saw tremendous growth, driven by the city's White residents. In fact, the city's White population shrank nearly 17% from 1950 to 1970. "Downtown," wrote Brookings, became "a place to be avoided, rather than the economic center of the region." During the 1980s, the number of Chattanooga's residents employed in manufacturing plummeted 28%. This was a place once called the "Dynamo of Dixie," already economically vibrant at the time of the Civil War (thanks to steamboat commerce along the Tennessee River). Capturing it was thus a key strategic objective of the Union Army, many soldiers from which settled there after the war. Decades earlier, it was part of the Cherokee Nation, until the Trail of Tears in the 1830s, when Andrew Jackson forcibly exiled the Cherokee to Oklahoma. Chattanooga's economy really took off with the launch of railroad service to Cincinnati in 1880—this was the first rail link reconnecting the north and south after the Civil War. Now a major transport hub, iron foundries and textile mills flocked to the city. Even as it boomed, however, the surrounding Appalachian region remained extremely poor well into the 1930s. It was then that President Roosevelt's New Deal program established the Tennessee Valley Authority, or TVA, which brought affordable electricity to a large portion of the South. It also, importantly, mitigated Chattanooga's deadly cycles of floods and droughts through a network of dams. Now supplied with cheap electric power, the city's industrial might expanded, becoming a major steel producer, for example, and a key provider of military material during the First and Second World Wars, as well as the Korean War. In 1933, only 2% of the Tennessee Valley had electricity. By 1945, the figure was 75%. Chattanooga's industry did make it one of America's most polluted cities, which contributed to its post-1950s population decline. Factories, meanwhile, continued to close after World War II, pressured by overseas competition. At least one local resident, however, believed in a Chattanooga comeback. Jack Lupton, heir to the world's largest Coca-Cola bottling company, sold it in 1986, reinvesting large sums of the proceeds in the city's economic development (not unlike what the Walton family is doing in northwest Arkansas, if on a smaller scale). Working with city planners, Chattanooga began reviving downtown areas, building, for example, an aquarium, a minor-league baseball stadium, new bridges and several hotels. The surrounding Cumberland Plateau and Appalachian Mountains, as it happens, make Chattanooga an attractive destination for tourists, helping to relieve the economic pressure from lost manufacturing. The TVA remains the nation's largest public power utility today, and the Chattanooga metro's fourth largest employer behind only three large hospitals. And speaking of hospitals, the area's health care economy is growing in tandem with its growing ranks of retirees. The U.S. retiree population, remember, is surging, which makes attracting seniors a powerful economic development strategy. Chattanooga's picturesque setting, helpfully, is a major lure, just as the reviving downtown has lured many millennials. Businesses, meanwhile—and remote workers—are lured by what the city advertises as the country's fastest broadband internet speeds. Tennessee is one of just nine states without a personal income tax. And if that's not enough of a lure, Chattanooga itself has offered unique incentives, including a $10,000 mortgage credit and $1,250 in cash for tech workers who move there. The metro remains a major transport hub thanks to multiple interstate highways and proximity to the booming metros Nashville and Atlanta, both only two-hours away by road. It's why Amazon has multiple fulfillment centers in the region. It's why some call Chattanooga the trucking capital of the U.S., home to firms like U.S. Xpress and Covenant. And it's why even manufacturing is coming back. In 2008, Germany's Volkswagen chose Chattanooga for a $1b auto plant that opened in 2011. It's now expanding to produce electric vehicles as well. Volkswagen's arrival birthed a cluster of auto suppliers, including a Spanish axle maker that's building a new $42m factory. Far from a dying place anymore, the Chattanooga metro is growing again, boosting its population 7% during the 2010s. That's not Nashville-like growth (*its* population jumped 17% last decade). But it matches the 7% growth in Knoxville and beats the 2% growth in Memphis, Tennessee's other major metros. The Chattanooga metro, to be clear, remains rather small, with fewer than 600,000 residents. Many still leave for better job opportunities in Nashville and Atlanta. Its nonstop air service is mostly limited to a few hubs like Atlanta, Charlotte, Dallas-Fort Worth and Chicago. The city's mayor, speaking recently to Bloomberg BusinessWeek, acknowledged the problem of lingering racial inequity. But make no mistake: Chattanooga's problems today are far less daunting than they were in the dark decades of the late 20th century. The city is now hoping to hit another development home run with a plan to build a new downtown baseball stadium for its minor league team. Thanks in large part to Volkswagen, manufacturing is back to a healthy 13% of employment, nicely balanced by roughly similar percentages for government, leisure/hospitality, professional services, education/health and the wholesale/retail trade. That sort of diversification is good. Really good.

MERCER COUNTY, NEW JERSEY

June 2022

I t's one of the wealthiest places in America. It's one of the poorest places in America. Can both statements be true? At one end of Mercer County is the town of Princeton, home to the world-famous university, multi-million-dollar homes and perfectly manicured lawns. Median household income: $146,000. Twenty minutes south is New Jersey's state capital Trenton, once a thriving industrial center but today a shadow of its former self. There you're in a different universe, one blemished with decaying infrastructure, dilapidated housing stock, bleak architecture, untended weeds, corner liquor stores, few places to buy fresh food and (in 2020) the seventh highest murder rate of any city in the country. Median household income: $37,000. In Princeton, 85% of residents over 25 have at least a bachelor's degree. In Trenton, the figure is just 14%. A quarter of all Trenton adults never even graduated high school. Princeton and Trenton are both older than the United States itself. Indeed, Trenton was already a thriving commercial center in 1776, when George Washington attacked a garrison of British mercenaries there—just after his famous Christmas crossing of the Delaware River. Days later, the Americans won the Battle of

Princeton, driving the British from what was already a college town. Nassau Hall, damaged during the battle, still stands on Princeton University's campus today. In the nearly 250 years since Washington's heroics, Princeton has maintained its status as an elite university town. And while some such towns have struggled (think New Haven, Conn., home to Yale), others like Princeton have been among the biggest winners in the modern U.S. economy. They're factories for knowledge in a knowledge-based economy. They're all-star teams of intellects from around the world. They're beneficiaries of high-priced tuitions subsidized by federal education loans. They're also bastions of wealth. Charlie Eaton, author of "Bankers in the Ivory Tower: The Troubling Rise of Financiers in U.S. Higher Education," cites Stanford economist Raj Chetty and his estimate that the top 38 private colleges today enroll more students from the top 1% of the nation's income spectrum than from the bottom 60%. Princeton University, for the record, is a private sector non-profit institution, with an endowment fund worth nearly $40b. Trenton, by contrast, is typical of the kind of place that's fared dismally in the modern American economy—one located in the northern quadrant of the U.S., previously dependent on manufacturing, depopulated by suburbanization and today home to primarily communities of color. Roughly 50% of Trentonians identify as Black or African American. Nearly 40% identify as Hispanic (note that some people identify as both). In Princeton, just 6% of the population is Black and 6% Hispanic. Both places have lots of foreign-born residents (30% of all Princetonians and 23% of Trentonians). But foreigners in Princeton tend to have much higher levels of education. Mercer County, to be sure, is more than just resplendent Princeton with its utopian University and struggling Trenton with its government jobs. The county, located roughly midway between New York City and Philadelphia, has a total of 12 municipalities, five colleges and universities and roughly 370,000 people. Government and education jobs aside, Mercer County benefits from tens of thousands of high-paying jobs in what's surely New Jersey's most strategic industry: Pharmaceuticals. After Princeton University, Bristol-Myers Squibb is the county's top private-sector employer. It's joined by other large drug manufacturers like Syneos Health, Janssen (owned by Johnson & Johnson), Aurobindo and Covance. No less important to the area are jobs in the FIRE sector (finance, insurance and real estate). Bank of America has a large corporate campus not far from Trenton's smallish airport (offering Frontier Airlines flights primarily to Florida). Blackrock, the world's largest fund manager, has a major presence as well, just across the highway from NRG, a large energy firm. Being so close to New York and Philadelphia, it's no wonder that Amazon operates large fulfillment centers in the county, employing roughly 4,000 people year-round (and more during holiday peaks). Capital Health, a hospital, itself employs nearly 3,000 people. Other sizeable employers include New Jersey Manufacturers Insurance, Educational Testing Services, McGraw Hill and Church & Dwight (owner of the Arm & Hammer brand). The plethora of high-paying jobs makes for some of America's most prosperous municipalities, which in New Jersey have heavy influence over public school funding. Well-funded and well-regarded public schools, sure enough, attract many highly educated immigrants from around the world, most notably India (the area's top source of arrivals) and China. Just under half of Mercer County's STEM workers are immigrants, according to New American Economy. Close to half of its construction and manufacturing workers are foreign born as well, many from Guatemala, Haiti and Ecuador, and many residing in and around Trenton. Unaffordable housing, a national problem, is certainly an issue in the prosperous towns of Mercer County, keeping low-wage workers out and many others fleeing the state in search of lower living costs (including lower taxes). Retirees—a growing demographic across America—have an added incentive to flee New Jersey's high cost of living since most no longer have use for its high-paying jobs or high-performing schools. Lower taxes in Pennsylvania or Delaware are a draw for some. Others prefer to escape the harsh northeastern winters and wet springs, opting for the Sun Belt. Mercer County, sure enough, lost population between 2014 and 2019. But the immigrant population grew 10%.

PUEBLO, COLORADO

June 2022

Pittsburgh and Bethlehem in Pennsylvania. Gary, Indiana. Cleveland, Ohio. Birmingham, Alabama. The history of America's steel industry was largely written in the country's eastern half. On the western side of the Mississippi though, just before reaching the Rocky Mountains, is another so-called "Steel City." Don't confuse Pueblo, Colorado, with Denver, currently one of America's fastest-growing economies. Pueblo bears zero resemblance to the affluent ski resorts of Aspen or Vail. Colorado Springs, a 45-minute drive to Pueblo's north, has an economy shaped by the U.S. military. On the western slope of the Rockies is Grand Junction with its shale gas. Back east is Boulder with its large university and high-tech jobs. Greely has its cattle industry. The area around Florence has its prison industry. Not Pueblo. There, the story is steel. As early as the 1880s, when settlers came to Colorado looking for gold, expanding local railroads badly needed steel for their rails. What better place to a put a mill than Pueblo, along the Arkansas River (part of the mighty Mississippi River system). Steelmaking requires a lot of water, often in short supply in the west but abundantly available in Pueblo. For much of the next century, the steel-producing

Colorado Fuel and Ironworks (CF&I) would employ more Coloradans than any other private company, bringing prosperity to Pueblo. The company provided steel not just for the nation's railroads but other infrastructure as well—the Brooklyn Bridge was built with steel from Pueblo. In 1920, the company employed more than 15,000 people. Like in the rust belt towns of the east, however, dependence on steel would spell doom in the final three decades of the 20th century. Labor strife, foreign competition, environmental regulations, the deep recession of the early 1980s, the nation's economic shift from manufacturing to services… all conspired to drive CF&I into bankruptcy by the early 1990s. Despite a seven-year labor strike, the mill stayed intact, purchased first by a company in Oregon and—just before the recession of 2008-09—the Russian steelmaker Evraz. In 2015, according to the Alliance for American Manufacturing, one of the mill's largest customers—the Union Pacific Railroad—decided to import most of the steel it needed from Japan. In 2018, however, the U.S. placed a 25% tariff on imported steel, giving the Pueblo steel mill a new lease on life. Union Pacific returned as a customer, and Evraz announced a new $500m mill alongside the existing facility—the new facility too, will focus primarily but not exclusively on the railroad market. Interestingly, it will get its power from an adjacent solar farm, currently the largest solar project east of the Rockies. But what about the plant's ties to Russia? So far, there's been no impact from sanctions, even those targeting the Russian oligarch Roman Abramovich, who owns 29% of Evraz. Pueblo officials worked hard—and provided financial incentives—to get Evraz to build its new mill in town, rather than in another location. In the meantime, Pueblo is trying to foster other industries to complement steel making, which these days is less labor intensive than it once was. Evraz will nevertheless employ more than a thousand people when the adjacent mill opens next year. According to the Department of Housing and Urban Development, it's just the sixth-largest employer in the area, with the familiar trifecta of health care, education and government dominating the upper ranks (Pueblo's single largest employer is the Parkview Medical Center). Some Pueblo residents commute to Colorado Springs for work, or to nearby Florence, home to a maximum-security federal prison housing some of the country's most infamous criminals (i.e.,

9/11 conspirators, the Boston Marathon bomber, El Chapo and other such lovely folk). Many commute the other way too. Pueblo's cheaper housing, combined with remote working, has led to a jump in new residents moving from Colorado Springs and even Denver. That said, Pueblo's average new home prices rose 15% last year, to $346,000 (that's after rising just 5% annually during the 2010s). Officials see economic potential in the cannabis industry. There aren't any ski slopes to attract tourists, nor even great views of the mountains. But nearby lakes and parks, plus a downtown riverwalk, generate some tourist income. A climate with 300 days a year of sunshine doesn't hurt when attracting retirees, including military retirees from Colorado Springs. Once a magnet for immigrant jobseekers flocking to the steel mills, Pueblo today has a population that's merely 3% foreign born. About half of the city's 112,000 residents are Hispanic, and about 4% Native American. Just 20% have college degrees, compared to 50% in Denver County. Per capita incomes, accordingly, are barely half what they are in Denver. Pueblo County's total population grew 5% during the 2010s. The unemployment rate is high by national standards: 5.1%, and above 6% earlier this year. Still, that's a long way from the near-25% unemployment that plagued the city during the steel crisis of the early 1980s. Pueblo today remains a town uncomfortably dependent on steel—owned by Russian interests, no less—but rightfully thrilled to see the sector's local expansion—powered by renewable solar energy, no less.

DETROIT, MICHIGAN

June 2022

He could have chosen 1913, when Detroit was fast becoming an economic superstar—thank the auto industry boom for that. He could have chosen 2013, when Detroit filed for bankruptcy—blame (in part) the auto industry gloom for *that*. Instead, journalist David Maraniss chose to write about Detroit at the midpoint of those two years: 1963. His book "Once in a Great City" depicts the Motor City at its pinnacle. GM, Ford and Chrysler were selling more cars than ever. Motown music was all the rage. The Civil Rights movement was advancing. The United Autoworkers union was gaining strength. And Detroit was America's fifth-largest city, surpassed in population only by New York, Los Angeles, Chicago and Philadelphia. But even as its star shined brightest, the Motor City's vulnerabilities began to show. Maraniss chronicles Detroit's boiling racial tensions in the 1960s, culminating in severe riots during 1967. Wealthier White residents and manufacturing facilities began to flee for the suburbs. Inadequate housing was a major issue. Union battles with the automakers intensified (and grew costlier). Presaging the despair to come, Detroit narrowly lost its bid to host the 1968 summer Olympics, which instead went to Mexico City. The New

Yorker magazine, reviewing the Maraniss book, likened Detroit in the early 1960s to "Humpty Dumpty's most poignant moment being just before he toppled over." As late as the final decade of the 1800s, nobody could have imagined the industrial colossus Detroit would become. It was always destined to have some commercial significance given its location along the Great Lakes, something its first settlers recognized in the 1700s. The Erie Canal boosted the town's fortunes in the 1820s. Railroads turned it into a manufacturing center, large enough to become America's 13th most populous city by 1900. Then along came Henry Ford, born on a farm in what's today part of Detroit. In 1903, he incorporated the Ford Motor Company, selling a car he called the Model A. Five years later came the immensely successful Model T, produced in mass quantities at affordable prices thanks to Ford's pioneering use of assembly lines. Though notorious for his bigotry, Henry Ford staffed his giant, vertically-integrated factories with European and Arab immigrants, farmers from Appalachia and—for the most menial jobs—African Americans escaping the Jim Crow South. In 1910, according to historian Ken Coleman speaking on NBC News, Detroit's Black population was less than 6,000 in 1910 but 120,000 by 1930, and 300,000 by 1950. Migration, indeed, both domestic and international, helped Detroit become the fourth largest city in America. The Great Depression, to be sure, was painful—GM cut half of its workers between 1929 and 1932, notes the Michigan League for Public Policy. But the 1930s gave way to a triumphant 1940s, when Detroit's auto factories helped build the tanks, jeeps and planes America needed to win the second World War. The 1950s brought cheap gasoline, a big increase in demand as more females began driving, the construction of new highways, the onset of suburbanization and a golden era for the Big Three. In 1963, as Maraniss recounts in his book, Ford and its brash young marketing chief Lee Iacocca was hard at work developing the Mustang, which would become one of the best-selling vehicles ever. During the 1970s, however, Detroit's fortunes rapidly reversed. Oil was suddenly expensive. Japanese automakers enticed Americans with fuel-efficient cars. Suburban flight accelerated. More factories moved out of Detroit, if not to the suburbs, then to the south, or overseas. David Halberstam in his book "The Reckoning" describes the highways and parking lots of Houston filled with Michigan license plates—a sign of people leaving the dying auto economy for the booming *oil* economy. The Motor City was still the country's fifth-largest city as late as 1980. By then, however, the U.S. economy was already reorienting away from manufacturing, in favor of service sectors like finance, health care, education, government and tourism. When the economy boomed in the 1990s, it was partly thanks to another era of ultra-cheap oil. Detroit's carmakers responded with popular trucks and SUVs, boosting their financial standing. But the real action was in places like Silicon Valley with its information technology, New York City with its finance and tourism, and the Sun Belt with its housing boom and population growth. Chicago too, Detroit's midwestern neighbor, would offset its manufacturing woes by becoming a hub for knowledge-intensive jobs and a magnet for tourists worldwide. By this time, it wasn't just Detroit's White population fleeing the city, but its middle-class Black population as well, many even moving back to southern cities their parents and grandparents fled. They helped, for example, turn Atlanta into a quintessential 1990s boom city, on display during the 1996 Olympics. Whatever modest momentum Detroit did regain in the 1990s, it was anyhow lost in the dismal 2000s. Another runup in oil prices, ongoing competition from Japan and Germany, growing concerns about climate change, skyrocketing pension and health care obligations, a giant financial crisis in 2008… all conspired to drive GM and Chrysler into bankruptcy, kept alive only with a federal bailout. At its peak in 1950, 75% of people living in the Detroit metro area were living in the city itself. By 2010, one year after the GM and Chrysler bankruptcy filings, the percentage was just 39%. The nation's fourth most populous city had become its twenty-fourth. Parts of its surrounding suburbs, to be clear, remained extremely affluent, growing with knowledge-intensive professional jobs—doctors, lawyers, auto executives, teachers, accountants, engineers, software developers, hospital administrators, etc. Today, health care and education employ more people in metro Detroit than auto manufacturing. That said, Ford, GM and Chrysler (known today as Stellantis) are still the area's top three private employers, in that order. The city itself though, with fewer and fewer people, had little choice but to itself file for bankruptcy in 2013. A third of its residents (roughly three quarters of them African American) lived below the poverty line. The city's debt was about $18b. Abandoned houses. Broken traffic lights. Rampant crime. Failing schools. You get the picture. Fortunately, the story starts to get better from here. The bankruptcy proceeding helped put the city of Detroit in a more fiscally sustainable position, to the point where it was even able to borrow in the bond market—without any state government guarantees—in 2018. For the first time in decades, a sizeable number of people began moving back to the city. Leading the charge was Dan Gilbert, arguably Detroit's leading business figure today. He's got nothing to do with the auto industry, but rather the housing industry—he's the founder of Rocket (formerly Quicken), America's largest mortgage lender. Gilbert's companies currently employ about 20,000 people downtown. Other important employers include Wayne State University and the College for Creative Studies, a top design school. Detroit's baseball, football, hockey and basketball teams all play downtown. Detroit will get a new bridge to neighboring Canada in 2024, to relieve traffic across the busy Ambassador bridge (which in normal times handles more than $300m worth of cross-border trade every day). The entire metro area, meanwhile, which lost 3% of its people in the 2000s, at least grew by 1% in the 2010s. The University of Michigan in nearby Ann Arbor is a critical economic institution. So is Detroit's airport, a major Delta hub with nonstop flights to Europe and Asia. The federal government, including the Post Office, employs about 30,000 people in metro Detroit. And the automakers are reinvesting again, with GM for one refashioning its Detroit assembly plant as the launchpad for its electric vehicle strategy. Chrysler currently employs nearly 5,000 workers at its Detroit factory. In 2019, it announced a $1.6b investment in the facility, which is located within the city. Manufacturing still represents about 13% of all employment in the wider metro, down from 16% in 2000. The unemployment rate is down to 5.5%, and much lower in the suburbs—metro unemployment was 17% in 2009. The city itself remains troubled, with the lion's share of new investment concentrated in relatively small areas of downtown, itself challenged by the work-from-home phenomenon. The pandemic of course didn't make things any easier. A semiconductor shortage is making life tough for automakers. But the Big Three are nevertheless financially healthy and hiring, allocating at least some of their giant EV investment spending to their home city. It's not 1963 anymore. But nor is it 2013. Perhaps in another 50 years, Detroit will again be an economic superstar.

CUMBERLAND COUNTY, NORTH CAROLINA

June 2022

Cumberland County, North Carolina: When *you* have an emergency, call 9-1-1. When the President of the United States has an emergency, *he* calls 9-1-0. That's the area code for Fayetteville, North Carolina, home to the U.S. military's XVIII Airborne Corps, along with the 82nd Airborne Division. At any moment, when duty calls, teams of highly trained soldiers are ready to deploy anywhere on earth within hours, by land, air or sea. They're based at Fort Bragg, which happens to be the largest military base in the world, housing not just the Airborne Corp but also U.S. Army Special Forces Command—think Green Berets and the Delta Force. Fort Bragg is in fact headquarters for the entire U.S. Army. The Air Force has a presence there as well and, all told, some 50,000 active-duty military personnel are stationed at Fort Bragg. Include family members, along with Defense Department officials, military retirees and military contractors, and Fort Bragg's population reaches something like a quarter of a million people. No wonder why some call it "Pentagon South." Naturally, the fort shapes the economy of Fayetteville and the surrounding areas of Cumberland County. The federal dollars paying for military wages alone is enough to support service businesses throughout the county, to speak nothing of the area's 850-plus military contractors. According to the Fayetteville-Cumberland County Economic Development agency, the community benefits from roughly $1.5b to $2b worth of military contracts per year. That makes for less cyclicality. The giant military footprint, furthermore, makes Cumberland the fifth most populous county in North Carolina, itself the ninth most populous state in the U.S. The base first opened in 1918, at the end of World War I. It grew sharply during the subsequent World War, followed by the wars in Vietnam and Korea. The pace of growth slowed in later decades. But periodic base realignments mostly resulted in *more* responsibility for Fort Bragg, not less. A 2005 realignment put Pope Air Force Base within its command. That's also when the U.S. Army Forces Command and the U.S. Army Reserve Command were relocated there. More recent Pentagon moves have added new units, while concentrating more of the Army's leadership and special forces there. That has Cumberland County forecasting healthy population increases for the coming decade, having grown about 5% last decade. Unsurprisingly, Cumberland County has more veteran-owned businesses than almost anywhere in the country. But it also has—according to economic development officials—the highest percentage of Black-owned businesses anywhere in the country. Black home ownership is relatively high as well. That's consistent with the military's history of being an important force for Black economic and social empowerment, dating back to President Truman's integration of the military after World War II, a move deeply unpopular in much of North Carolina at the time. Today, roughly 40% of Cumberland County's residents identify as Black or African American. More than 12% identify as Hispanic. And while only 6% are foreign born (compared to 14% nationwide), the area has an international feel given the military's global responsibilities—there are some 85 languages spoken in the local school system, including mother tongues from places like Afghanistan and Iraq where the Army has had extensive deployments. There remains, however, high levels of economic distress around Fayetteville despite all the Pentagon dollars pouring in. The county's poverty rate is close to 20%, compared to 13% nationally. College attainment is below the national average. The area, to be sure, hasn't seen the same sort of explosive economic growth taking place in North Carolina metros like Charlotte (with its banking), Raleigh-Durham (with its elite universities and booming IT sector) and Asheville (with its tourism and retirees). But at least it's adding people, which is more than you can say for about half of North Carolina's 50 counties. Fort Bragg aside, Cumberland County's health care and education sectors employ about a quarter of the local workforce. Amazon is building two distribution facilities, lured by Fayetteville's location along busy Interstate 95, midway between New York and Miami. The Norfolk Southern and CSX railroads run through. The deepwater port of Wilmington is not far. Goodyear Tire, Campbell's Soup and Cargill are among the manufacturers with production or distribution facilities in the county. Booming Raleigh is about a 1.5-hour's drive north, close enough for about 4,000 Cumberland residents to commute to jobs there each day (efforts are underway to establish an Amtrak link). The Fayetteville airport, meanwhile, though small, actually gained new flights during the pandemic, a testament to the economy's relative resilience during the crisis, aided by the steady flow of Pentagon dollars. To be clear though, the pandemic did hit hard, especially in the service sector. Another challenge for local businesses is competition with the military base, which features its own entertainment and other facilities catering to troops and their families. In addition, the base, along with other big employers like hospitals and colleges, are exempt from taxation, straining local government resources. A challenge for the housing market is the transient nature of military personnel, who often remain at a given base for only a temporary period. On the other hand, a large nearby military base implies a young demographic overall, and many retirees with unique skills. Robert Van Geons, President and CEO of Fayetteville-Cumberland County Economic Development, is leading the charge to recruit more residents and businesses to the area. Golfing and nearby parks help with attracting retirees—the mild winter weather doesn't hurt either. Efforts are underway to improve broadband infrastructure. Downtown Fayetteville is seeing more investment. Crypto mining, notwithstanding the sector's current troubles, is prevalent in the county. It's the Pentagon though, that dominates the economy.